A how-to guide for women wanting to get ahead in any walk of life, drawing on the experiences of those who've done the hard yards. *Helen Clark ONZ SSI PC*

Read and be inspired. Read and take courage. Read and with renewed confidence, Take Your Space. *Mavis Mullins MNZM*

TAKE YOUR SPACE

SUCCESSFUL WOMEN SHARE THEIR SECRETS

JO CRIBB and RACHEL PETERO

OneTree
HOUSE

Ehara taku toa i te toa takitahi

Engari, he toa takitini

My strength is not mine alone

but due to the strength of others

Take Your Space acknowledges the strength of all women who came before,

who stand today, and who will take one step forward tomorrow.

First published 2020

ISBN 970995117662

Produced by: OneTree House Ltd

Cover Illustration: Vasanti Unka

Design: Vasanti Unka

Edit: Anna Golden

10 9 8 7 6 5 4 3 2 1   0 1 2 3 4 5/2

Printed in New Zealand: Wickliffe powered by bluestar

CONTENTS

FOREWORD

You could sometimes be forgiven for thinking gender equality in New Zealand is well within reach. Three of our past five prime ministers have been female, as have our last two chief justices and three of our last six governors-general. Kiwi women reaching the peak of their chosen profession – be it in the world of sport, fashion or literature – is no longer front page news.

But just as we should rightly celebrate our success stories, we shouldn't ignore the fact that women are still too often underappreciated, underpaid and underrepresented. They still face significant barriers in many areas and entrenched societal practices mean they are also often expected to carry a larger domestic burden than men. The result? For all the progress of recent decades, too many women are still being held back from reaching their full potential.

No one knows this better than Jo Cribb and Rachel Petero. Both are former Women of Influence finalists – an annual awards programme co-presented by Westpac NZ and Stuff – that celebrates women who are driving change, and showing others how they can do the same. This is what makes Take Your Space such a tremendous resource - it identifies issues women face in the workplace and offers practical help.

Drawing on their experience as managers, mentors, advocates and organisers, Jo and Rachel know the questions on the minds of Kiwi women. How do I stand up for myself in the workplace? Who should I look to for guidance? Which sacrifices are worth making and which aren't? But they also have some answers, and in the following pages they share them in an engaging, no-nonsense way, with stories from a range of inspiring Kiwi women who've refused to be held back.

One of the guiding principles within Westpac NZ is that diversity of people leads to diversity of thought and diversity of ideas, and I know Jo and Rachel share that view. We're proud to support these trailblazing Kiwi women, and we hope their book will start many more Kiwi women on the path to success stories of their own.

Gina Dellabarca
Head of Consumer Banking and Wealth
Westpac New Zealand

INTRODUCTION

We have much to celebrate – women hold leadership positions across the globe with much lauded success. And yet, no country has or is likely to achieve gender equality anytime soon. More men named Mark or John head companies than women. Globally, for every dollar a man earns, women earn 77 cents. One in three women will experience violence in their own homes… You know the stats.

Some of us have been able to go to 'Women in Leadership' events, paying thousands of dollars for a ticket. We have a day or two off work and learn how we can succeed. But only certain women have access to this advantage. Only certain women are able to go to such events and to speak at them – those who have jobs that will pay for them to go. For most of us, we will miss out on this opportunity to learn the secrets of other women's success.

Rather than throwing our hands up in despair or whining over a wine, we have decided to take the matter into our own hands. We don't think women need fixing. We think women are fabulous. But we know that it is not a level playing field out there. And times are tough, and likely to get tougher. Until things improve, until the playing field is level, we will need to work harder and smarter to succeed, and we are going to have to support each other and share what we have learnt to get ahead.

There are women succeeding on their own terms. We wanted to know how they are doing it. We wanted to know the practical steps they took, and the life and career hacks that worked. We wanted to collect all of this and then share it as widely as possible. You deserve this information, these secrets.

We also want all women to be able to access this information, and to celebrate successful women leaders in all their glorious diversity. By women, we mean all people who identify as women (this does not necessarily mean they were born girls). We know about ethnic pay gaps, about the lack of Indigenous women in decision-making roles, the missing voices of our disabled sisters and our side-lined LGBQT+ friends.

So think of this book as a group of women sharing a bottle of wine or a pot of tea together. In the spirit of generosity and openness, they share what they have learnt the hard way. Think about these women as women who want you to succeed. Think about them sharing their frustrations, anger, sadness, and laughing hard together with you.

Think of us as your cheerleaders…

Our aim is that you will get ideas about actions you can take to move forward and succeed at whatever success looks like for you. Our hope is that you have the tools and the confidence to ask for a pay rise tomorrow, or to get that job you really need.

We have a not-so-secret ambition: if all of us did some of the actions in this book, there would be a tidal wave of change.

Sharing secrets to get ahead

We started this project by researching the most common barriers to women getting ahead, and we identified eight. Each of these is a chapter.

Value Your Worth
We look at your attitudes towards money, how to work, how much you should really earn, and how to negotiate for a pay rise.

Take Your Space
We share tips on how to get heard in meetings, how to get your ideas taken seriously, and how to influence others.

Take Off
We share strategies to get promoted, appointed to new jobs or boards, and (if you are a business owner) funded and invested in.

Own Your Confidence
We focus on exactly what is says because keeping and building confidence in yourself can be an ongoing battle.

Make Work Work
We show you how to negotiate flexible and part-time work arrangements.

Stand Up for Yourself
We give you strategies to deal with harassment, sexism and racism.

Give and Take
We focus on how to negotiate sharing house and child-work.

Put Your Mask on First
We look at how you can take care of your mental and physical wellbeing.

We interviewed 14 women and, on your behalf, interrogated them for the secrets to their success.

We divided up the drafting (the power of working together) and in each chapter we start by sharing our experience. Then we share some stats and evidence. Some of you will know it already, if so please skip past this section. We will not be offended; in fact we celebrate how smart you are in using your time well. For other readers, this will be new data. We have summarised what we think are the most relevant facts. We have read all the books and boring journal articles so you don't have to. There are references as well if you want to learn even more.

The focus of this book and more than half of each chapter is what *you* can do to get ahead. This is the purpose of the book. Too often we focus on describing the problem and don't get around to taking action. Not here, not in our book. We outline the best hacks and actions we and our women have found. You don't need a PhD or to buy anything to take our advice (though you might want to invest a fancy new notebook – but we like stationery and don't think that's a bad thing). You will need courage and determination.

Meet your hosts

If this is like a morning tea or drinks party, then think of us – Rachel and Jo – as your hosts. We want to put you at ease, make you comfortable and we want your time with us to be as meaningful as possible. So let us introduce ourselves, like good hosts do.

RACHEL PETERO

Rachel Petero is the Founder of Rise2025, a global consultancy aiming to reimagine the futures of 100,000 Indigenous women and their whānau by 2025. She is an Entrepreneur by heart, a HR and Executive Coach by profession, and Waikato-Tainui by whakapapa. She advocates and drives gender equity, diversity and inclusivity through her leadership roles in governance, business and community development.

Rachel had fifteen years international commercial experience in London, UK and Doha, Qatar before returning home to Aotearoa, New Zealand in 2015. Through her corporate business development and governance experience as Co-Chair of Te Ohu Whai Ao Trust and Ngāti Tamaoho Charitable Trusts, Rachel continues to remain locally grounded and globally focused.

With partnerships in Samoa, Canada, Chile, Australia, Middle East and North America she also maintains Cultural Advisory roles with Sysdoc and Otara Bluelight. As a board director for UNICEF New Zealand, she believes Aotearoa can lead the world in equality. Rachel's husband John, is Cook Island, Tongan and Niuean.

JO CRIBB

Jo is an experienced consultant. She is regularly asked to facilitate strategy sessions with leadership teams, coach emerging leaders and lead substantial policy, strategy and gender projects. Recent assignments include facilitating sessions at the Commonwealth Heads of Government (CHOGM) meeting and working to increase diversity in the New Zealand Defence Force.

She is a director on a number of Government and NGO boards (including the New Zealand Media Council, Royal New Zealand Navy Leadership Board and Institute of Public Administration of New Zealand (IPANZ). She is a regular media columnist on gender issues and part-time lecturer at the Australia and New Zealand School of Government (ANZSOG).

Jo was a previous Chief Executive of the Ministry for Women and former Deputy Children's Commissioner and leader of the Commissioner's Expert Advisory Group on Solutions to Child Poverty. She has a doctorate in public policy that investigated the contracting relationship between governments and NGOs, and a management degree from the University of Cambridge, UK.

More importantly, she is a proud mum to two kids and distills her own gin.

Meet your cheerleaders

So we have invited you and 14 other women to come together to share. We know it can be intimidating walking into a room where you don't know anyone, so let's introduce you to the group.

ALEXIA HILBERTIDOU

Alexia has one focus for her life: to support girls and women. She founded GirlBoss New Zealand with a single mission: to close the gender gap in science, technology, engineering, maths, entrepreneurship, and leadership. Working with her network of 13,500 young women, she and her team empower and inspire young women to lead and change the world.

Talking with Alexia, you get a sense that this is a young woman who is prepared to march on the path less travelled to make a difference. She chose not to go to university in favour of growing GirlBoss New Zealand. This journey has seen her speak at the UN and at One Young World in London, the biggest youth conference in the world, and will undoubtedly take her wherever she wants and needs to go in the future.

ANJUM RAHMAN

Anjum might describe herself as an accountant, but as the Project Lead of the Inclusive Aotearoa Collective Tāhono, community leader and human rights activist, she is making an impact so much wider than any balance sheet.

Born in the Indian state of Uttar Pradesh, she moved with her family to New Zealand in the early 1970s. She has been actively engaged in politics, standing for Parliament in three elections.

She was a spokesperson for the Muslim community following the Christchurch mosque shootings in 2019 and voiced her frustration at the failure of the New Zealand government to take concerns about violence towards the Muslim community seriously. She has made submissions to select committees on behalf of the Islamic Women's Council in support of gun law changes. For her tireless work, she was awarded Queen's Birthday Honours for her services to ethnic communities and women in 2019.

ANN FRANCKE

Following a meteoric rise through global corporate brands, including Procter and Gamble, Mars and Boots UK, Ann is a global legend in marketing. But in talking with her, it is her latest career reinvention as the Chief Executive of the Chartered Management Institute in London that is providing her with the opportunity to bring all the strands of her career together.

In this role, she has done extensive work in promoting gender equality and effective leadership in the workplace. Her book on gender balance was published in 2019. Before that, Ann authored the *Financial Times Guide to Management* and was named in the top 100 women to watch in the 2015 *Female FTSE Cranfield* Report. She was awarded the MemCom award for outstanding leadership of a UK professional body in 2016.

Ann holds several board positions and five honorary doctorates for her work in management and leadership.

ARIZONA LEGER

Arizona describes herself as an enabler and a team player. In talking with her, it is clear the global stage will be where she will find her team. In 2019 she was selected from thousands of applicants to speak at the Girls20 Global Summit in Japan. There she connected with a wide range of youth leaders about a range of issues.

She is a child of New Zealand and Oceania, proudly representing her tribes of Ngāpuhi, Ngāti Kuri, and Ngāti Hine on her mother's side and her Samoan, Tongan and Fijian heritage on her dad's side.

Arizona has a powerful voice that she fearlessly uses to speak and inspire and challenge. As Head Girl of Epsom Girls' Grammar School, and with a background in communications and media studies, she is regularly called on as a keynote speaker and youth leader.

BRENDA TRENOWDEN

Success for Brenda is having a loving family. Her two kids, husband and dog are her source of strength and happiness.

Success for Brenda also includes the work she has been doing leading the 30% Club as its Global Chair. Established in 2010 with the initial aim of achieving a minimum of 30 percent female representation on FTSE 100 boards, she can happily report they have helped achieve that. Her focus is now on supporting more women into senior management to shore up the leadership pipeline.

Brenda's professional background is in banking, having worked for some of the biggest global institutions.

BRIDGET FOLIAKI-DAVIS

Born and bred in Auckland, New Zealand, Bridget started working as a waitress but spent more and more of her time in the kitchen. By the age of 20, she was a fully qualified chef with a young daughter. At age 22, she had her own business in Sydney, Australia, and by age 23, she had two separate businesses and kitchens operating at either end of the city.

Today she works as restaurant consultant for new businesses, owns and operates two gastro pub kitchens, works as a culinary demonstrator, cooks on cruise ships as a chef entertainer, and works as boutique caterer and presenter for Google. She presented at TEDx Sydney on technology, social media and how it affects food culture. As an online influencer, brand ambassador and technology expert, she now no longer has time to work in commercial kitchens.

EDITH AMITUANAI

Edith's parents came to New Zealand from Samoa in the 1970s. Her extended family and immediate community are the subjects for her photography. She focuses on intimate portraits that explore the concept of home. She sees the world through images and she is always looking to see where people grew up, neighbourhoods and homes.

Her first solo exhibition was in 2005 and she was the youngest artist to have been included in the publication *Contemporary New Zealand Photographers*. She has participated in a number of high profile group exhibitions around the world. She gained a masters in fine arts from the University of Auckland's Elam School of Fine Arts, has won many awards, and has taught in the tertiary, secondary and primary sector.

JACKIE CLARK

Jackie describes herself as a force of nature who has a strong sense of social justice. Everything in her life has led her to her current role – running the NGO, The Aunties. The Aunties works with women, often referred from social agencies and who have escaped violent relationships, to provide them with what they need to get back on their feet, be it food, clothing or a trip to the movies.

With a background as an early childhood educator for 20 years, her interests lie in the empowerment of women, especially young women of colour. Her joy is to see them claim their space and their own power.

In 2018, Jackie's work was recognised with a Queen's Honour, and she was the Supreme Winner at the New Zealand Women of Influence Awards.

KRISTEN WORLEY

Kristen is a world class cyclist who challenged the highest levels of international sport on science, gender and human rights and won. Born of a New Zealand mother adopted and growing up in Canada to a conservative family, sport played an important part in Kristen's life. Growing up as a boy, she became enmeshed in a personal struggle to understand her true self, search for her identity and find acceptance. Cycling became an important tool day-to-day and integral to her survival. She made swift progress at national level and set her sights on the Olympics.

A crash and serious injury put her cycling career on hold and meant she needed to face her gender dysphoria. As she transitioned and pioneered, she battled global sports officials to seek fair treatment of female athletes who have transitioned, based on the abuse and impact of gender testing of women worldwide in the elite sporting system. Kristen's book 'Women Enough' tells her epic journey and how she found a way forward.

LINDA JENKINSON

Linda is a global entrepreneur and mother from Aotearoa New Zealand. She systematically and successfully scaled $100 million companies, and is a magnet for business talent. Linda is an entrepreneurial pioneer and visionary.

She was the first NZ woman to list a company on the NASDAQ stock exchange with DMSC, the $250 million on-demand courier company she co-founded, that was described as being like Uber before Uber. She went on to establish a global customer and employee experience platform, which was sold to the Accor hotel group, and WOW for Africa, which is an NGO supporting women entrepreneurs in Senegal.

She sits on multiple boards including the boards of Air New Zealand, Guild Group and Massey University. She was named EY Master Entrepreneur of the Year New Zealand in 2013, and named World Class New Zealander in 2016.

Based for many years in hilly San Francisco, she now calls Wellington home. She's known for her warmth, irreverent attitude and sense of adventure. She says she's often mistaken for the tea lady.

ROYAL REED

After working for law firms in New Zealand and Australia, Royal hit the glass ceiling so she established her own practice in Hamilton in 2006. Responding to increasing demand from the migrant communities for bilingual legal services, Royal moved to Auckland and transformed her firm.

She is a regular a public speaker and social media influencer, giving many pro bono legal information sessions both in New Zealand and overseas. She is involved in many other volunteer activities and has received numerous honours and awards, including the 2016 ANZ Migrant Support Award and winner of the Highly Commended award for Community Service in Law at the 2012 NZ Law Awards.

SARAH JANE MOON

Sarah Jane Moon is a painter who specialises in portraiture and figurative painting. Her work explores identity, sexuality and gender. She has exhibited with the National Portrait Gallery, Royal Society of Portrait Painters, Royal Institute of Oil Painters, New English Art Club and the New Zealand Portrait Gallery, among others. In 2015 she was awarded the Arts Charitable Trust Award and in 2013 the Bulldog Bursary for Portraiture. She has also been included in the Pride Power List, which celebrates the achievements of notable LGBTQ people and is a regular supporter of Stonewall UK, Terrence Higgins Trust, Pride in London and Art for Youth.

Originally from New Zealand, Moon has lived in Japan, Malaysia, Australia and UK, working in education and the arts. She has qualifications in art theory and curatorial practice from Universities in NZ and Australia, as well in portrait painting from the Heatherley School of Fine Arts in Chelsea.

STACEY MORRISON

Stacey is a New Zealand television and radio host, with a varied career spanning 25 years. She is married to TV presenter Scotty Morrison, and they have three children together.

Stacey speaks fluent te reo Māori, though didn't learn to speak until she was an adult. She and her husband Scotty wrote *Māori at Home* to help other families use te reo in everyday settings, Stacey has written *My first words in Māori* and they both work with many groups and families to build Māori-language friendships and community for whanau. Stacey has been an advisor on pre-school and children's TV shows, which, along with her experiences with her own children, has helped her identify the words children pick up early in their language learning. As a winner of Te Taura Whiri i te Reo Maori Champion Award in 2016 and a graduate of Te Panekiretanga o te Reo (the Institute of Excellence in Māori Language), Stacey loves encouraging the learning and use of our country's beautiful native language.

TRACI HOUPAPA

Traci grew up as one of four children on a sheep and beef farm in Te Rohe Potae - the King Country, in New Zealand's North Island. Her whakapapa includes German, Croatian, Waikato Maniapoto, Taranaki and Tūwharetoa.

In her early career, Traci was encouraged by her kaumatua to take on a range of roles to gain lived and learned experience, including working for a Māori Trust Board as operations manager and then as chief executive. She later gained an MBA from Massey University which complemented her business experience and achievements. She is now a professional direction, serving as a Chairman and director on a number of boards.

Traci is an award winning director, as well as a recognised industry and Maori leader. In 2012 she received an MNZM for services to business and Māori in the Queen's Birthday Honours, and in 2015 won the Board and Management award at the New Zealand Women of Influence Awards. She has also been named on Westpac's New Zealand Women Powerbrokers list. In 2016, Traci was awarded the Massey University Distinguished Alumni Service Award for services to New Zealand agribusiness and Māori, and named as one of the BBC's 100 Most Influential Women in the World.

VALUE YOUR WORTH

– Jo Cribb –

* Check your attitude towards money
* Work out how much you should earn
* Negotiate a pay rise
* Invest in your future skills

I was angry and felt betrayed when I worked out I had been paid tens of thousands of dollars less than my colleagues doing similar roles. In total, probably enough to buy a house.

I was in my twenties when my manager was seconded to another role. The GM offered me the opportunity to 'act up'. I got an 'acting-up allowance' (a small percentage increase in my base salary), and when my permanent appointment went through this became my permanent salary. On leaving the role several years later, I worked out how little I was paid compared to the other management team members. I had trusted that my manager, the government department, and the public service would treat me fairly. Wasn't the public service all about transparency, fairness and merit?

However, Rachel learned quickly not to under-value herself in a competitive male dominated overseas market. Her male colleagues told her to 'do as the Romans do' if you want to be considered as an equal. So she charged exactly what they did, learnt to negotiate her value through shadowing the best and copying success. Throughout all of this she remained true to her Indigenous values and worldview. Rachel added, 'If my ancestors were trading in the 1800s across the world, why wouldn't I?'

Unfortunately, many of you will have had similar experiences to me and aspire to learn to negotiate like Rachel.

You are not alone

Women are consistently paid less than men. Worldwide, women only make 77 cents for every dollar earned by men. This means globally women need to work more than three months more each year to earn the same, more if they have children. At the current rate of progress, it will take more than 70 years for women to be paid equally[1].

The median income of a woman in New Zealand in 2019 was 9.3 percent less than the median income of a man and it has stubbornly remained about the same for the past decade[2]. Australian women earn on average $241.50 per week less than men; a 14 percent gender pay gap[3]. British women can sort of celebrate. Their gender pay gap is high at 17.8 percent but it is on a steady decline[4]. It is oo soon to break out the champagne just yet.

These gaps can look like a bunch of boring statistics but to me they tell the stories of women whose pay packages are smaller, who will struggle to provide what they would like for their kids, to save for their retirement, or have a financial cushion should the washing machine breakdown. These numbers talk to me about their ability to put food on tables, pay for school uniforms and bus fares.

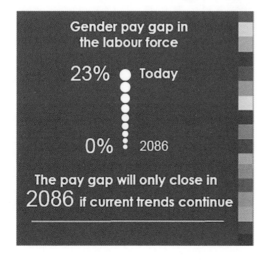

Gender pay gap in the labour force

23% ● Today

0% ⋮ 2086

The pay gap will only close in 2086 if current trends continue

What is emerging from the research on the gender pay gap is the role of discrimination.

The reasons why there are gender pay gaps are clear.

One is *occupational* or *horizontal segregation*, which is a fancy way of saying that men work in industries that are paid more. Industries that employ predominately women (such as clerical and sales) do not attract high salaries.

The other is *Vertical segregation,* an equally fancy term that simply means that even when men and women are employed in equal numbers in an organisation, usually more men than women are in the higher paying managerial positions. Ladies, we congregate in the lower ranks with the low salaries.

Then if we have children, and take the bulk of responsibility for childcare, we may collect the motherhood penalty which means when we seek flexibility we may sacrifice our wages or salary and promotion opportunities.

Twenty or so years ago, the gender pay gap could be explained by women having fewer qualifications and skills. Now, this is only a small cause of the gap as many women leave higher education with more qualifications than men. The impact of horizontal and vertical segregation is also declining.

Now, almost two-fifths (39 percent) of the gender pay gap is attributed to direct and unconscious gender discrimination[5]. It is the most significant current factor that drives our smaller pay packets.

> *I had my second child while was in my first law job. I was working from 8am to 7.30pm most nights and taking work home. I had a contemporary who was a gym addict. He would arrive at one minute to 9 and leave at one minute to 5 for his gym sessions. He was a young, white boy who was quite fun.*
>
> *I was bringing in more than 500 clients a year. He didn't bring in any.*
>
> *By the time I was in my second year of the job, I was given a bonus of a Venetian blind installed in my office, so I could breastfeed my baby when she had to come into the office some days. He was given a massive promotion to the position of associate. Immediately after that he moved to a very big firm, just because someone else that went to the same gym asked him to 'come over'.*
>
> *When I eventually left that firm I was told by the partners at my farewell that it felt like a goldmine was walking out of the door, and they were sad about it. But when I was there, I felt like I was treated like child with special needs, not a goldmine by any measure.* **Royal Reed**

Pink Tax

While we might be as qualified, when we reach the workforce we are less likely to be hired, given training opportunities, talked up, or promoted. Even if we had the courage to ask for a pay rise, we are less likely to be successful than our male colleagues[6]. And our Christmas bonuses, you guessed it, are smaller by half. UK research shows 55 percent of companies have a bonus gap higher than 30 percent, more than double the gap for our salaries[7].

All this is happening in relative secrecy. Though some countries have passed laws that mean companies have to publish their aggregated pay data, many women work in countries that have not. This means we usually do not know if we are being paid fairly.

We are also unlikely to talk about our pay. A British survey found that women would rather talk about our weight, our sexually transmitted infections, and family fights than how much we earn[8]. The New Zealand Commission for Financial Capability found that more than half of couples do not talk to each other about how much they earn or spend and do not talk about money with their children[9].

Instead of talking to them, we leave it to the media to educate our kids about money. In the UK press, 70 percent of articles that were aimed at men portrayed men as the money makers, and financial wealth as key to personal status. In contrast, 70 percent of articles about money in women's magazines showed women as excessive spenders who cut coupons to make ends meet[10]. Such gender stereotyping about money starts early. The most popular children's books of the last decade consistently show Dad relaxing after doing a hard day of (real) paid work, with Mum in the kitchen[11].

Then when we take our smaller pay packets shopping, we face the *pink tax*: the extra amount we are charged for products and services marketed specifically to women and girls. Examples of this include deodorants, shampoos, shaving products and services like dry cleaning, haircuts and even car repairs. Just because the deodorant bottle has a flower on it and a 'feminine' fragrance is no reason for it to cost more. That floral bottle might have less work to do than the Lynx Tobacco and Amber scented one right next to it on the shelf.

One fabulous contributor, experienced not only the pink tax but also the high financial cost of the social expectations on women for clothing and grooming and professional workplace when she transitioned.

> *Twenty years ago [when I transitioned], I changed my clothing, especially my professional clothing. I've learnt that a high percentage – and I'm very conservative – of my expenses now go into my day-to-day living, and my clothing and just general care of myself, whereas somebody born as a male just needs a couple of suits and you're good to go.* **Kristen Worley.**

The real kicker is that if we try to rectify this and try to negotiate more money, or seek promotion, we are labelled as ambitious or aggressive. These are not compliments. So we try to be nice, to please everyone, and get overlooked. So that strategy doesn't work either.

I still struggle around that kōrero [negotiating for more pay]. I don't want to demand more money because I trust that this is what you think I'm worth, and therefore if I push, I am breaking this imaginary trust that I've created between you and me.

I signed my first contract without reading it. I didn't look at it. I trusted that it was going be all good. Learning about contract negotiation for me has been massive, because the next job I went into, I was there sitting, reading every word. I had learnt the hard way what it meant to not be fearless in those conversations and to be too trusting. **Arizona Leger**

Over our lifetime, the impact of earning less, taking time out, caring for others, and not being promoted (not to mention divorce, where we lose out financially) means that when it comes to retirement, we face a significant retirement savings gap.

RETIREMENT GAP Grim. So, let's do something about it.

Australian men aged between 30 and 60 currently have 42 percent more retirement savings than women of the same age[12]. The average woman retiring in New Zealand in 2017 did so with $80 000 less savings than a retiring man[13] and the gender gap in savings is growing. One in six British women are expected to retire on incomes less than that needed for an acceptable standard of living[14]. In Australia, almost 40 percent of retired single women live in poverty. Older single women are now one of the fastest growing groups of people living in poverty.

Here's what you can do
Drawing on the experiences of our 14 women, there is a range of things we can do to ensure we value our worth and do not get ripped off.

START BY CHECKING YOUR ATTITUDE TOWARDS YOURSELF

I know it sounds like something off a cheesy birthday card, but to value your worth, you have to value yourself. For Anjum, this meant overcoming her childhood experiences and the message she consistently got that she was not valued.

> *My experience of growing up was being told I wasn't a valuable person. It has been a fight for me: to accept that I have value. I feel like a lot of the community work that I've done is my way to try to make myself valuable.* **Anjum Rahman**

We need to give ourselves permission to be awesome. The way the world is now, we need everyone who has talent and the desire to solve problems to be out there doing so. We don't have the luxury of sitting back and hoping others will sort everything out or wait for someone to ask us to contribute. We need everyone who can make a difference to be right in the mix getting stuff done. But it can be hard if you feel like you are not enough, always on the back foot, stretched a million ways, never doing anything well.

> *I've had constant internal dialogue around what it means: not being enough, not doing enough. Personally, for me, I think it comes from the different 'va' or space that we as women (wahine) have to occupy. Whilst you may think you're enough in the workspace, usually that means you've lost your va as a daughter, or as a wife, or as a sister. When you can feel enough in one space, it's very easy to feel not enough in another. I struggle to find that balance a lot of the time.* **Arizona Leger**

It can be even harder if we are focused on what we have not achieved, or what is still on the To Do list, instead of reminding ourselves what we have actually achieved. At the end of a rough week, our sole achievement might be that we still have a pair of clean underwear left. That in itself is something to celebrate.

THEN CHECK YOUR ATTITUDE TOWARDS MONEY

As I was writing this heading, I started to write: *attitude towards money and wealth*. But the W word seemed a step too far. Wealth. Wealth. Wealth. There I have typed it three times but it still feels uncomfortable, like an expensive stiletto pinching my toe.

Each year when the rich lists come out, there are less than a handful of women on them. Those that are there are usually part of a family business. It has been called the 'diamond ceiling'. Women just don't control the world's wealth.

Is it because we do not want to grow our businesses to scale? That we are happy with our lot? Is it because amassing large fortunes isn't something we really care about? Is it because there are so many barriers to overcome for women growing big businesses? Whatever it is, the statistics around women and wealth haven't changed much over time and seem unlikely to budge[15].

But who wouldn't want to earn well, to provide for those you care about, and give yourself and those your care about more choices?

The Australian Financial Attitudes and Behaviours Tracker (2017)[16] found just that: 46 percent of women reported they found dealing with money stressful and overwhelming. Many women reported low levels of financial confidence. Men are more likely than women to have reported that they agreed with the statement 'Dealing with money is interesting' and most of us women don't even know how much savings we have for our retirement.

A large British survey[17] found that there are four ways that women look at money: money as power (status spender), money as generosity (generous indulger), money as security (secure saver), and money as freedom (independence lover). In all of these we can have unhealthy ways of thinking about and using money. The most common are worrying all the time about how much you spend, buying things to feel better, and being in denial about spending habits. Seeing money as security helps reduce the risk of money problems, while seeing money as power increases the risk.

SO, IT IS IMPORTANT TO CHECK YOUR RELATIONSHIP TOWARDS MONEY— WHAT DOES MONEY MEAN TO YOU?

Most importantly, you need to check your attitude towards making money. For three of our women, coming to terms with the fact that it was more than okay to earn and earn well was hard but very important to their future health and well-being.

Sarah Jane, a self-employed artist and teacher, was raised to never talk about money. But in the art world she needs to set her own prices. Through listening to audio books about money she started to realise how unhealthy her relationship with money was. She then challenged herself to believe that it is okay to want to make money; she is actually running a business and needs to behave as such.

Stacey grew up with similar attitudes towards money. She felt she didn't deserve it or was not worthy of money (and rich people were wankers anyway). To overcome this, she sought professional advice from a financial advisor and put in place a plan for her and her whanau (family). Success for her isn't about being rich, it is ensuring her family are provided for.

Anjum questions how we often conflate money with success – if you don't have money, one can be assumed to be lazy or incompetent. She also questions the myth that she thinks middle class people share: that everyone has the same opportunities available to them. By buying into this myth, those who have enough can be comfortable about there being those who don't. She strongly values her ability to be financially independent, which proved important when raising her children as a single parent.

Jacki strongly advises us not only to think about our attitudes towards money but also the attitudes of our partners. Working with women who are escaping violent relationships, she sees the role money can play in unhealthy and unsafe relationships.

In every relationship there is a power dynamic that's slightly askew. My estimate is that 70 percent of women, trans, gay or cis hetero are in relationships that are unhealthy. If your relationship's unhealthy, money becomes a problem because it becomes another thing to argue about.

I spoke to a 75-year-old woman the other day, she was in quite a wealthy couple. She was looking to get out of the relationship, but he pays her $1,000 pocket money a week. And she's 75. There's an alarming amount of women who are younger than that who are similarly stymied.

One of my friends said, 'I'm very chill with money and so is he, and he's really bad at money and so we just spend our money together. But everything goes in and everything goes out of that one account.' And others have got separate accounts. But in general, I think women don't like to take control of money at all or they end up paying more. I know I did. My husband paid the mortgage and I paid the bills, the food. But the bills and the food were worth more every month than the mortgage. I think that's not unusual. **Jackie Clark**

If you are struggling with your attitude towards money, especially about whether you deserve to have money, four of our women have advice for you.

For **Bridget**, her change in attitude came when she realised being a successful businesswoman meant she could employ and help her family members. For her, generating wealth was about creating wealth not for her, but for her wider family.

Similarly, **Stacey** acknowledges her Māori Indigenous culture, which focuses on collective wealth, not the wealth of the individual. Earning money and generating wealth is a service to the wider family, and is about providing for current and future generations.

Edith sees having money as an opportunity for generosity, the more she has the more she can share.

For **Linda**, money is freedom. She has experienced making and losing money. By creating money, she created the space to be truly herself.

I have made a lot of money and lost a lot of money and made a lot of money. The first time round I didn't like it at all. I found that I actually didn't want money. I was 30, and I didn't like the way people treated me. I found it very objectifying. People made judgements about me, which I didn't like. It felt very disconnected.

A realisation I had was that money isn't really money – money is really freedom and opportunity. By creating money, I created the space to truly be myself. Money's not the object – it's just a tool. It's a great tool to have. **Linda Jenkinson**

So let's ditch our imposter syndromes and the voices in our heads that say we are not good enough or worthy of our salaries. Each year in your role you become more experienced and more valuable to your employer. You have and will continue to build your knowledge and skills. You have contacts and relationships that mean you can get more work done. You know how the systems work. You know where things are in the stationery cupboard. It would take serious money to replace you, with your knowledge and contacts. It makes so much sense for your employer to pay you, and pay you well.

So let's also stop being the polite girls with pigtails who were rewarded for being good at junior school. Let's stop being too nice, trying to please everyone, only sharing our views when they are asked for and putting up with 'just okay'. What worked for us in junior school is not working for us in the workplace. You don't need to be evil; being nice enough is good enough – and being nice enough includes asking for what you want and what you deserve.

Being nice enough also means you have worked out the line between when you are being kind, generous and giving, and when you are being taken advantage off.

Traci learned the hard way, through near exhaustion and collapse, that putting your own well-being and well-fare first is important. Being physically, mentally and financially fit means Traci is in in the best position to support her family and fulfil the many leadership and governance roles she holds.

Stacey is clear about how important service is to her – service is part of herself, it is giving back to her people. But she found that she has been taken advantage of, usually by corporates who will take her time without thanks or acknowledgement.

Getting comfortable saying no, was **Alexia's** lesson. She evaluates what most benefits her cause and has learnt to prioritise, and say no.

> *I charge as a professional public speaker. For a good couple of years I honed my craft and spoke for free, and there are a few charities which I support now, but for a corporate audience, yes of course I charge. The caterers, venue hire and event organisers are all paid, so the speaker should be too. I have learnt that if you don't value your time, neither will others. It's important to value what you know and value what you have to give - and don't be afraid.* **Alexia Hilbertidou**

FIND OUT YOUR WORTH.
So now we have convinced you that you are worthy of money, even wealth (see I am getting better at using the W word), we need to help you find out just how much you are worth.

Start by focusing on what you are good at and what you contribute to your team and organisation. Think about what problems you have already solved and how many colleagues' work lives are better because you are there. If you are self-employed, think about the value you bring to your clients. If you are in a caring or unpaid role, think about the value you bring to those you look after. This will focus you not on what you think about yourself but on your value to your organisation and others.

Then get business like. Find out where you sit on your organisation's pay band. Understand your organisation's pay and promotion policies and criteria. Then try and work out how your role fits, as well as defining the role you actually play (your job description and what you actually do are often different).

Then focus on data collection. Ask your union representative or colleagues what they are paid. If this is a step too far, ask what different roles are paid in your organisation rather than asking individual people. **Jackie** recommends asking what your male colleagues are paid first. Statistics show that they are likely to be paid more. Include in your data collection information about bonuses and other perks.

If data collection from inside your organisation is too hard (and it is likely that it will be), **Brenda** recommends talking to headhunters and recruitment agencies. Ask them what a role like yours is usually worth. Check out job ads and job websites to work out what is being offered for roles like yours.

Stacey's message to you is to not be surprised if you find discrimination (that is, you are being paid less than others in your organisation or for the market rate for your job). In her experience (and the gender pay gap data shows), we are not all paid equally.

NOW NEGOTIATE TO GET WHAT YOU ARE WORTH.
Some of us get a opportunity each year during a performance review to initiate a negotiation for more pay. If you have the opportunity, take it seriously. Each performance discussion is an opportunity for you to highlight what you have achieved and pitch your worth to your employer.

Traci recommends calling on mentors, coaches and colleagues to help you prepare. She has a number of 'truth tellers' that she regularly seeks advice from. These confidantes provide her with clear advice and support. With them, she can role play discussions or scenarios, get objective advice on how to deal with issues and opportunities, and get second opinions as needed. You will need to be an advocate for yourself, so having help and support to do this is critical.

For **Ann**, preparation for pay negotiation should happen all year. She recommends keeping an achievement log. In this, keep notes of what you deliver as you deliver it, and notes about the impact of your work. Include feedback you have received and mentions of your work or projects. Think about it as a running tally of your value to your organisation. You will need to include enough detail so that you can show evidence of what you have achieved in your performance review.

Doing this will not only help you realise how competent and valuable you are, it also means you will never be caught off guard or unprepared when the opportunity comes to seek more pay or a promotion. You will be able to use your achievement log to demonstrate how you have achieved what is expected off you (from your work plan or job description), and to show if and when you have achieved more than expected.

If you don't have a formal meeting each year, or you want to negotiate your pay because you are ready to, arrange a meeting to do so. Be clear about the purpose of the meeting and that you want to talk about your pay. Never ambush your manager. It never ends well.

Before you enter the meeting, put yourself in your employer's shoes. How is s/he likely to respond? What authority does s/he actually have to act on your request? What is happening in your team and in their management roles? Plan your conversation thinking about your audience and what will be most convincing for her/him.

In your meeting, make your case logically and with evidence. Show what you have achieved, focusing on what is over and beyond what was expected of you. Outline what value your work has brought your organisation. Think about what is happening in your organisation. Perhaps there are projects coming up that you know you will be able to add value to, so include an argument about the future value you will bring. State what you found in your research about other people's pay rates. Then ask.

Before your meeting, perhaps when you are practicing it with 'truth tellers' consider what your response will be if the answer is no, or not now. What is your Plan B? If you don't get a raise, are there other things you want (flexible hours, opportunities for training or secondments)? This will mean you will maximise your conversation even if you get a no straight off. If you get a no, a second prize (like a training course) might be goer.

HOW TO NEGOTIATE A PAY RISE.

SIX STEPS TO GETTING WHAT YOU ARE WORTH:
1. Ask 'critical' friends to help you prepare
2. Do your homework (market data, your achievement log)
3. Use your annual review or ask for a specific meeting with the purpose of reviewing your pay
4. Think about your boss' perspective
5. In your meeting, use evidence and logic
6. Know what your Plan B is

Remember to stand your ground. Remind yourself of what you have achieved. Know that there are thousands of women who have your back. We want you to succeed.

If you are finding the conversation hard, why not focus on doing it for the young women that are coming next, or for your colleagues who don't have the confidence, not for yourself. When I feel intimidated, I focus on 'we' rather than on 'me'. For me, the desire for my daughter to be free of the rubbish we have to put up with now makes me fearless. It's like a secret super power (though obviously not so secret now).

Keep your negative thoughts in check. If you start to think, 'what if s/he thinks I am pushy? What if my boss won't like me anymore because I am asking for more money? What if I am labelled a trouble-maker?' nip them in the bud. Quick. You can do this.

Or move to plan b.
Royal worked out that she could ask her employer for more money until she was blue in the face. She could see she had been put on the mummy track with a large sprinkling of racism. She was not going to be valued or treated fairly so she left and started her own business.

> *I was considered such a liability because I had little ones, though the little ones hardly ever interfered with my ability to work.*
>
> *By moving to self-employment, I charge my own hours and am paid on my terms. In the last ten years since I started my firm, many different law firms have offered me rates that I could never have imagined if I had stayed loyally working for someone else. Even if I worked for many years, my previous employer would never have realised my real worth.* **Royal Reed**

Royal is very aware that not all women will be able to start their own business. But she has advice she shares with her young women recruits: do not become too specialised. She encourages them to think about creating skills and opportunities outside law that they may wish to draw on in the future. She sees great value in ensuring women have a number of avenues to earn and don't become trapped in one firm or in one narrow field of expertise.

INVEST IN YOURSELF.
'Think hard about your skills, the knowledge and competence you have, and how you are building and investing in yourself,' is great advice from **Anjum**. As she sought a career in politics and to advocate for communities facing discrimination, she invested in media training as part of her preparation.

For **Linda**, it is being aware of what the world is telling us we can and can't do, and then not listening.

> *I was at a conference with lots of women and the conference organiser puts some math on the board. He puts up 2 + 2 x 4 =. Then he says, now I want you to break into groups of 20 and talk about this. We come back 20 minutes later and the facilitator goes, 'Okay, before anyone says anything, I want you to put up your hand if you know the answer.' I put up my hand. I am the only person of 200 who puts up their*

hand. He then asked if everyone had been told at school that they were no good at math. As soon as he said, 'We're doing math,' everyone said to themselves, 'I can't do it.' They didn't even try. Linda Jenkinson

Being told you are no good at something is one of the most destructive messages one can receive, and so often we are not even aware we've received it.

HERE'S HOW WE CAN HELP EACH OTHER.
While this chapter has focused on you – and rightly so – there are also things we can do to support and encourage each other, things that value <u>our</u> worth.

If you control a budget or hire people, are you paying everyone fairly and are the resources in your budget used to support both men and women equally? Pay equity starts with you.

Those of us in positions of influence, who are sitting around decision tables, have the opportunity to advocate for pay transparency. We have the means to encourage organisations to share their pay data and data about their gender and ethnic pay gaps publicly. When organisations do this, it makes it easier for their workers to know that they are treated fairly. It takes out the step about having to research your pay.

We can all have a role in breaking the taboos about money. We *can* talk about money with each other, and with our children. We can study up about money and be active in all decisions about it.

How To Checklist - Value your worth

- **Check your attitude to money.** Do you really think you are worthy of being paid well? If your answer is no, starting working on challenging and changing your relationship to money.

- **Focus on what money can do for those you care about.** If you are struggling with your attitude towards money, focus on 'we' rather than 'you'. Money can bring security, freedom and opportunities for those you care about.

- **Pay yourself first.** You need to be financially fit before you can help anyone else.

- **Research your worth.** Turn detective. Work out what your job is really worth by studying pay scales, policies, job websites and talking to recruitment firms.

- **Keep an achievement log.** All year write down what you deliver, what the impact of your work is, and what people are saying about your work. Use this as evidence for your performance review and to remind yourself how awesome you are.

- **Walk in your boss's shoes.** Think about what value you bring to your boss and what problems you solve for him/her. Use this thinking about your boss to plan for your performance review and pay discussion.

- **Ask.** Just do it.

- **Have a Plan B just in case the answer is no**. What do you want instead? After a no, you are in a great position to get a yes. Or if the answer is no, is it time to polish up your CV?

- **Break taboos about talking about money.** These taboos result in some women being paid less than they are worth. Talk to your friends and partner about money. Talk to your kids about money.

Endnotes

1   UN Women https://www.23percentrobbery.com

2   https://www.stats.govt.nz/news/gender-pay-gap-unchanged-since-2017

3   https://www.wgea.gov.au/data/fact-sheets/australias-gender-pay-gap-statistics

4   https://www.ons.gov.uk/employmentandlabourmarket/peopleinwork/earningsandworkinghours/bulletins/genderpaygapintheuk/2019

5   https://www.dca.org.au/research/project/shes-pricedless-2019-update-report

6   https://www.dca.org.au/sites/default/files/shes_pricedless_-_detailed_report_0.pdf

7   https://www.wgea.gov.au/newsroom/latest-news/bonuses-drive-up-gender-gaps

8   https://inews.co.uk/light-relief/offbeat/brits-would-rather-talk-about-their-weight-mental-health-and-family-dramas-than-money-539993

9   https://www.cffc.org.nz/news-and-media/news/money-week-2019-now-were-talking/

10 https://www.starlingbank.com/campaign/makemoneyequal/

11 Pollard, Clare (2019) Fierce Bad Rabbits: The Tales Behind Children's Picture Books Penguin RandomHouse, UK

12 https://www.smh.com.au/money/super-and-retirement/study-shows-retirement-savings-gender-gap-is-42-per-cent-20190416-p51ejn.html

13 Groom, Merewyn (2018) Beyond the Pay Gap: The Retirement Disadvantage of Being Female, Policy Quarterly, Volume 14, Issue 1, pages 64-67

14 https://www.moneywise.co.uk/news/2018-05-30/heres-why-women-retire-ps4900-year-less-men

15 https://www.noted.co.nz/money/money-business/why-arent-more-women-getting-to-the-top-of-business

16 https://financialcapability.gov.au/files/afab-tracker_wave-6-key-findings.pdf

17 https://www.bbc.co.uk/teach/the-test-what-does-your-attitude-to-money-say-about-you/zk4292p

TAKE YOUR SPACE

– Rachel Petero –

* Influencing and owning your space
* Making sure your voice is being heard
* Challenging social norms in all areas of society
* Taking action that moves you forward

My story began with a question from the Chief Executive Officer (CEO) of HSBC UK. He asked me, 'Where are you from?'

had already said I was from New Zealand so, feeling slightly annoyed, I repeated myself. 'I'm from New Zealand,' and then added, 'I'm Māori, Indigenous to New Zealand'.

He responded, a bit too energetically, 'Wow, I've never met a Māori from New Zealand before.'

As I take my space today, as a wiser and more worldly Indigenous woman, I know I should have replied, 'I come from a long line of warriors, leaders and innovators who traversed the world trading goods and services. I come from the rich soil of my tribal lands that were taken through war and colonisation. I come from the wisdom of ancient knowledge that can be traced back to before mankind. I come from survivors and a worldview that we are guardians, not owners of all things natural. I come from goddesses and my womb is where life is nurtured, so damn it, treat me as such. I come from dreams of a better future for generations to come. My name is Rachel Petero and yes, it is your lucky day to meet me.'

As women, we need to take our space, not only for ourselves but for all those young women following in our footsteps. You must make this about more than just you, and *take your space*.

The business I won that day at HSBC was their recruitment budget to advertise their jobs at monster.co.uk. I was new to my role as a key account manager with Monster, the worldwide market leader of online job listings, HSBC was one of my corporate clients. My role was to influence the key decision-makers in the corporate world to spend their recruitment budgets online, versus print.

It felt good to win that day. As I tagged along with the team to our 'regular' (code the pub on Chancery Lane – part of the work hard, play hard culture) to celebrate, I quickly realised that taking my space in this testosterone-fueled industry required a **winning game plan**.

Fortunately, I grew up playing games and wanting to win has always been a part of my competitive nature. Growing up in west Auckland, New Zealand, playing sport was non-negotiable. Rain, hail or shine I was out there; netball, softball, rugby, touch rugby, basketball were standard issue.

That day at the pub on Chancery Lane, feeling more confident after a few large glasses of Pinot Gris, I decided I'd be friends with the A-team at Monster. Sport had taught me to surround myself with people with different skills and strengths than me; to learn from them and apply their skills.

Next I realised I had a much bigger challenge. Women in the online recruitment industry were few and far between and all my corporate clients were men. As I met more industry experts at the copious social gatherings, events and awards, I noticed that women's voices were largely absent. My voice has always been my preferred mode of communication; Māori are orators, storytellers, performers, philosophers, singers, and musicians, and throughout my lifetime Māori and Indigenous speakers have inspired me to speak in many different spaces around the world.

Finding my voice in the online recruitment world, with its little regard for gender diversity (90 percent of sales staff were male), seething testosterone and massive egos, was challenging. It was enough to put anyone off and God help you if you showed emotion or broke down in tears. I chose not put up with any of that shit and to give back as good as the boys could dish out. My approach earned respect. My voice was heard alongside my new

A-team mates, Duchess, Jules and Butters. I was known as Patero (said with an English/Spanish twang).

In addition to a lack of gender diversity, cultural diversity was scarce – double whammy for me. At times it felt three times harder: a woman, ethnic and Indigenous. It felt like no one understood my cultural worldview, and conversations about feminism and diversity were not agenda items at weekly sales meetings. The All Blacks haka was as deep as anyone wanted to go.

My English mates saw me as a Kiwi. Yet I didn't look like the other Kiwis. My skin is chocolate brown, my nose is wide, my lips are full and the gap in my teeth is inherited. In New Zealand I'm Māori – in London I was exotic. The more diverse you are, the more labels you acquire. It's exhausting.

Throughout my two years with Monster I felt a deep inner strength knowing that my ancestors had walked and occupied this foreign land. They had stood in the spaces where I now stood. They had opened spaces around the world so that more Māori could take our space, wherever our journeys took us.

I'm reminded of one of my tribal ancestors, King Tawhio, the second Māori King, who travelled with a delegation to meet Queen Victoria in 1884.[1] These were highly political times between Māori and the Crown, and Te Tiriti o Waitangi (The Treaty of Waitangi) between the Crown and Māori had been dishonoured; Māori lives and lands had been lost at the hands of the Crown. Queen Victoria snubbed King Tawhio's visit in 1884, but that didn't worry our King. The treaty negotiations, the relationships between Māori and the Crown, started way back then and continue to this very day.

Silencing women – Stats and evidence

Throughout history, women have had to fight to have their voices heard. Yours may have been one of those voices silenced. Now more than ever it's time for your voice to be heard.

VITAL GOVERNMENT VOICES

Traditional governments worldwide have been dominated by a male narrative. UN Women estimate that globally, men still hold the majority of spaces and represent 77 percent of parliamentarians, 82 percent of government ministers, 93 percent of heads of government and 94 percent of heads of state.[2]

The importance of women's political participation has become increasingly vital as we raise our voices about universal issues that directly impact women, such as child poverty, domestic violence, housing, education, health and pay equity, to name but a few.

MICHELLE OBAMA   (wikimedia public domain)

Michelle Obama's political stand as the First Lady of the White House was education for all girls. She leveraged her political position to raise awareness globally for girls and education.[3] She is a role model for young black women and girls, highlighting the impact women can have in politics.

Clearly, when aligned to a cause greater than herself, one woman can change lives.

As women, we must no longer limit ourselves. Women's voices and our bipartisan approach to peace, justice, and national security are needed to influence all areas of policy and reform. Nirmala Sitharaman, India's Finance Minister,[4] and Australian Senator Linda Reynolds, the current Minister of Defence,[5] are examples of women leading in political spaces traditionally occupied by men.

The representation of women in government positions globally is on the rise in most developed nations. But at present only 24 percent of the parliamentarian seats in those nations are occupied by women, and in 2019 they represented only 5 percent of heads of government.[6]

But we know it's not only about the numbers. We need to see success in politics role-modelled by women. Quotas have been a key influencer of progress in women's political participation. Of the top 20 countries with the largest share of women in parliament in 2020, 16 apply some type of gender quota.[7]

Research and evidence tells us that gender politics matters when it comes to achieving broader outcomes for more sustainable, healthier, wealthier nations.[8] More women in government ensures there are diverse perspectives and decision making about 'who gets what, when and how resources and budgets are allocated.' Numbers matter.

New Zealand women have always fought to take their space in politics. Dating back to 1893, female activists like Meri Te Tai Mangakāhia and Kate Sheppard campaigned tirelessly as part of the suffragette movement for New Zealand women to be the first in the world to vote. One hundred and twenty-seven years later, New Zealand has our third female prime minister, The Right Honourable Jacinda Ardern, and 38 percent of the 120 members of Parliament (46) are women. This is the highest number New Zealand has ever had since women were first allowed to stand for Parliament in 1919.

% of MEN in Government

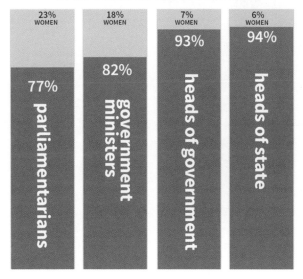

PERCENTAGE OF MEN IN GOVERNMENT
The male narrative is not serving our female voices.

Today in Rwanda, Cuba, Bolivia and the United Arab Emirates, women now account for 50 percent or more MPs in their lower or single chambers, compared with 1995 when no parliament had reached gender parity.

Owning our cultural spaces

Globally, as women step into political and corporate spaces, the reality is that ethnic women, women of colour, and Indigenous women remain silenced and marginalised to an alarming extent.

Discrimination affects most women at some time in their lives; women of colour, ethnicity and Indigenous women even more so. Diverse women, often the minority within a dominant work culture, are absent in leadership and governance roles. Globally, the higher you go the less diversity we see.

When you take your cultural space, you support more women to do the same.

The economic and social impact of being invisible has many repercussions

In Canada, Indigenous or First Nations women make less money, work in lower-level jobs, are less likely to find employment, than non-Indigenous women or Indigenous men. According to a national report by the National Aboriginal Economic Development Board of Canada, the economic impact of this is that Canada is missing out on a whopping $27.7 billion annually

1.3 MERI TE TAI MANGAKĀHIA   1.4 KATE SHEPPARD

because of its 'under-utilised' Indigenous workforce. The stats paint a grim picture for First Nations women, one which is replicated across many Indigenous nations. To influence change within your cultural context you must find models of success within your own history and bring this knowledge into the twenty-first century. The time is now.

For Australian Aboriginal women unemployment rates are three times the non-Aboriginal rates. Australia's *Closing the Gap 2018* report showed that nationally, the employment rate for Indigenous Australians has not improved over the past decade. Aboriginal women identify education and employment as intrinsically linked to economic opportunity. Aboriginal communities have suffered depravation as recently as 50 years ago, yet, as the world has witnessed, the influence of Aboriginal women on government, industry and education in recent years, confirms the power of women to write a new future.

In Aotearoa New Zealand, there is a different story forming for Māori women holding key positions, in government and business specifically. In government, 13 women MPs self-identified as having Māori affiliations following the 2017 election (10.8 percent of the total number of MPs). This compares with the average number of women overall (38 percent of MPs) following the 2017 election. The *Ngā wāhine kaipakihi: he tirohanga, Māori Women in Business: Insights* report found that 6,500 wāhine Māori in Aotearoa New Zealand run businesses across multiple industries. New Zealand history tells us that women can overcome any barrier. Role models like Meri Te Tai Mangakāhia, Dame Whina Cooper, Princess Te Puea Herangi, Te Arikinui Dame Te Atairangikaahu and many others are our examples of what is possible.

Meri Te Tai Mangakāhia, Dame Whina Cooper, Princess Te Puea Herangi,
Te Arikinui Dame Te Atairangikaahu

However, there is still much more to do. Across all Indigenous cultures women occupy spaces that disempower our intrinsic value. We must raise our voices, individually and collectively, to shine a light on the inequalities we face every day. I recently shone a light on a conference for women that was held in Auckland, New Zealand, which had zero diversity or cultural consideration. That one LinkedIn post is my reason for writing this book for you.

Challenging social norms

Despite progress in some areas, no country in the world (rich or poor) has achieved gender equality, according to UNDP's *Human Development 2020* report. Yet women matter to the economic, environmental, human, and social development of today's global issues. We hold the answers to the other half of the world's problems. How women influence and challenge social norms requires that all women be seen, heard, and counted, in every area of society.

The *Human Development* report's Gender Inequality Index (GII) measures women's empowerment in health, education, and economic status. Overall progress in gender inequality has slowed in recent years. Some of the reasons for this are hidden, unmeasured burdens that create barriers for women to move forward. Barriers like:

- **working your day shift and then working your un-paid shift at home,**
- **harassment in public places and on transportation,**
- **discrimination in workplaces,**
- **domestic violence,**
- **sexual harassment,**
- **cyber bullying.**

These are just some of the multiple hidden constraints that stop women from taking their space in all areas of society. Being aware of what is happening in different spaces around the world gives context and relevance to how you can influence change by seeing what works and noting what doesn't. When you collaborate for change with other women, our voices are more powerful and purposeful.

One of the ways we can measure progress in correcting social norms is through 17 Sustainable Development Goals.

1. No Poverty
2. Zero Hunger
3. Good Health and Well-Being
4. Quality Education
5. Gender Equality
6. Clean Water and Sanitation
7. Affordable and Clean Energy
8. Decent Work and Economic Growth
9. Industry, Innovation, and Infrastructure
10. Reduced Inequality
11. Sustainable Cities and Communities
12. Responsible Consumption and Production
13. Climate Action
14. Life Below Water
15. Life on Land
16. Peace, Justice and Strong Institutions
17. Partnership

Goal 5 – Gender Equality sets out to expose and eliminate all forms of discrimination against all women and girls everywhere. Yet globally, the facts tell us we have a way to go. Seven hundred and fifty million women and girls were married before the age of 18, one in five have experienced physical and/or sexual violence by an intimate partner, and only 13 percent of agricultural landholders are women, globally.

There is hope, when collective voices, are united for social impact. Social movements are influencing global collectives to speak out. Activism and demonstrations – including online campaigns, women's marches, and street performances – demand that society shine a light on human issues that impact women, which have previously been hidden.

Three global examples include:

1. **The #MeToo movement** – *This has given power to previously ignored women's voices, uncovering the abuse of power and privilege of thousands of women.*
2. **The #IWillGoOut movement** – *This demanded equal rights for women in public spaces in India.*
3. **The #MMIW Missing and Murdered Indigenous Women movement** – *This started in 2016 by demanding justice for 5,700 missing or murdered Indigenous women and girls across First Nations, Inuit, Métis (FNIM), and Native American communities.*

Challenging social norms in New Zealand is in our DNA. For example Dame Whina Cooper, of Te Rarawa, is best known for leading the famous 1975 land march from Te Hāpua (in the far north) to Parliament in Wellington, inspiring thousands of New Zealanders to stand and march together with her.

According to the Women, Peace, and Security (WPS) Index, which measures women's autonomy and empowerment at home, in the community, and in society across 167 countries, only one country (Iceland) performs well in every aspect of women's lives. Regionally the WPS Index data also shows where there are high levels of organised violence and discriminatory laws, often coupled with low rates of inclusion; especially in paid employment we see disempowerment of women and girls. Empowerment is the goal for women and girls because empowerment helps to activate safe spaces at work, in public, and at home. As Secretary-General Kofi Annan quoted, at the opening meeting of the 2005 UN session of the Commission on the Status of Women, 'study after study has taught us, there is no tool for development more effective than the empowerment of women.'

Kristine Bartlett, an aged care worker, partnered with her union to tell her life story as a single mum bringing up three children, earning $14.46 per hour for 19 years. Because of her selfless campaigning, 55,000 care and support workers received the biggest pay rise of their lives. The cost to the government in 2017 was NZ$2 billion. Kristen's voice became the catalyst for policy and legislative change. Social norms were changed forever.[9]

Valuing women in the arts and media

The arts, film and media industries continue to favour and promote men above women. Every second of the day, society is being exposed to gender-biased content that contains women and girls as stereotypical archetypes. On film, on canvas, on a smart phone or TV, these platforms have the ability to make or break women in a heartbeat. How we turn up and own these spaces is critical.

Edith Amituanai is an artist of the people and of her beloved Ranui (West Auckland) community. She is also the first Pasifika woman to hold a solo exhibition at Wellington's Adam Art Gallery, which she did in 2019. She shares:

I convinced my father to allow me to drop one subject to do photography, a non-certified subject at college in those days. My dad was really annoyed that I only took 'four subjects', but it didn't matter, because the thing that became successful in my life was that subject. I did have to push for that. If I [had been] a bit more of a people pleaser, maybe I would have done what he wanted. [But] I knew this was my life, this was my education. **Edith Amituanai**

In researching female artists in the US and Europe, only two artworks by women have ever broken into the top 100 auction sales for paintings, despite women being the subject matter for approximately half of the top 25. Women's artworks are significantly discounted compared with men's works at auction.

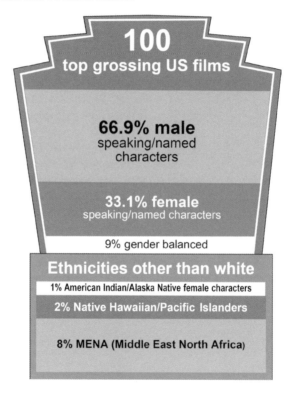

In London, UK, for example, 78 percent of galleries represent more men than women, while only 5 percent represent an equal number of male and female artists. Outrageous.

Of the top 100 grossing US films, only 33.1 percent of all speaking or named characters were women/girls. Only 9 percent of the movies had gender-balanced casts. Female characters from the following racial/ethnic groups were excluded: American Indian/Alaskan Native female characters (99 movies), female Native Hawaiian/Pacific Islanders (97 movies), and MENA (Middle East North Africa) females (92 movies).

Women in the arts, media or creative industries have been invisible or silenced for too long. Their voices carry significant value due to their ability to speak to the masses through the platforms they have access to. There are many examples of women lending their influential voices to social justice and reform through media, film and the arts, like Oprah Winfrey, Alyssa Milano, Ellen DeGeneres, Beyoncé Knowles, Frida Kahlo, Merata Mita, Lisa Reihana, to name a few.

One of our Māori media celebrities, Stacey Morrison, adds her voice:

> *I guess because my bent is media and communications, one of the things I have observed is the desire to shut women down. [It] is so natural to many men. Yes, to other women too. I just think that the way people respond to women who are strong and public is so much harsher … so harsh, and it goes straight to quite an abusive place. That just shows what you really think in terms of whose voice should be valued.* **Stacey Morrison**

Being heard in the boardroom

Historically, the corporate boardroom and top C-Level positions (CEO – Chief Executive Officer, COO – Chief Operating Officer, CFO – Chief Financial Officer, CMO – Chief Marketing Officer, CIO – Chief Investment Officer, etc.) have been off-limits to women. Generations of women have worked hard to advance their careers, only to be stopped at the boardroom door.

Globally, progress for women on boards is slow as Catalyst March 2020 research shows below. A Deloitte analysis of more than 8,600 companies in 49 countries showed women held 16.9 percent of all global board seats in 2018, up from 15 percent in 2016. The most disappointing statistic is that, of the 8,600 companies, only 5.3 percent of board chair positions were held by women in 2018.

Influencing boards in business to get your message across takes practice. Making sure you are clear on what you want to say, and having allies to back you up, means that preparation is key. When women understand the different communication profiles in a meeting or around a boardroom table it can be useful to pitch your message for a particular audience. If the decision-makers are highly analytical then providing the detail upfront will assist decisions to be made more easily. Understanding how men communicate will allow you to adapt your communication style as required.

Brenda shares her reality in business and on boards:

> *Being talked over still happens to me from time to time in meetings when there aren't enough of us. Once you get to three women on a board, then you've normalised [it] and you can start to be heard a bit more […] It is very hard if you're the lone woman. But one of the things I've learned from watching others, (and it's worked for me), is choosing some people in advance to discuss the point that you want to make and being a bit savvy about getting their support in the meeting.* **Brenda Trenowden**

A shift is required for equity to be realised on boards for women. That shift requires the voices of men, advocating and championing alongside women. The *Male Champions of Change* initiative in Australia, is a proactive establishment driving gender equity. In their 2019 impact report, direct CEO engagement is one of the Top 3 high-impact actions delivering gender equality, according to 100% of Chief Human Resources Officers polled. They are consistently creating data-driven results on women on boards, promotions, policy and parental leave to name a few of their results.[10] Activating and empowering all generations of men to take part in the next phase of mentorship, coaching and advocacy is paramount if we want to see equity and equality in our lifetime. And I love that men are leading the way.

Women's Global Representation on Boards, 2019

Country	% Women Directorships, 2016	% Women Directorships, 2019	% With 3 or More WOB, 2019	% With 1-2 WOB 2019	% With Zero WOB, 2019	Quota and Year Introduced
Australia	26.0%	31.2%	58.2%	40.3%	1.5%	No
Canada	22.8%	29.1%	63.0%	35.9%	1.1%	Pending
France	37.6%	44.3%	98.6%	1.4%	0.0%	Yes, 2010
Germany	19.5%	33.3%	81.0%	17.2%	1.7%	Yes, 2015
India	12.8%	15.9%	21.3%	78.8%	0.0%	Yes, 2013
Japan	4.8%	8.4%	3.4%	63.2%	33.4%	No
Netherlands	18.9%	34.0%	65.2%	34.8%	0.0%	Yes, 2013
Sweden	35.6%	39.6%	96.6%	3.4%	0.0%	Yes, 2016
Switzerland	17.5%	24.9%	48.8%	51.2%	0.0%	Pending
United Kingdom	25.3%	31.7%	82.2%	17.8%	0.0%	No
United States	20.3%	26.1%	56.2%	42.8%	1.0%	CA Only, 2018

Source: https://www.catalyst.org/research/women-on-corporate-boards/

So what can you do?
FINDING YOUR SPACES FOR SUCCESS

First, find spaces and environments where you can thrive. If your current role isn't doing it for you, find other spaces, including volunteering on boards of charities who are more aligned to your *why* (your personal values, your purpose or true North). Jo highlights ways to do this in Chapter One: Value Your Worth.

I encourage you to seek out different spaces that really make the most of all parts of you; your passion, your skills, your values, your connections, your time. I know firsthand that when everything aligns and you do what you love, it never feels like work.

If you want to make a difference and contribute to something you are passionate about, try:

- **preparing young girls in high school for the future of work**
- **helping mums returning to work to find their next career**
- **advocating for more women on boards.**

If you find you are on a stale, pale, male corporate board of financial services, great questions to ask yourself are:

- **Is this space fully utilising all my skills and passion?**
- **Am I energised in this space?**
- **Am I contributing and adding value?**
- **Who am I being in this space?**

One of our vibrant wahine (women), **Arizona Leger,** is an enabler of powerful conversations. She transitions from grassroots to mainstream TV, and on to the global stage seamlessly. When I interviewed Arizona she had consciously decided to work with and mentor young men, 13 to 18 years old, who had found themselves in the justice system for different reasons.

When I asked her about why she chose this mahi (work) at this time in her life, she simply said, 'my job at the moment is enabling them [young Māori and Pasifika men] to see life outside of crime… a lot of my mahi is about taking someone's perspective and enabling them to see past that.' On the topic of leadership, she adds:

> *Having that village mentality for me is massive – not only in that global space, but in any leadership space for me. [It] is understanding that if you've been called to be a leader, then you're obviously leading a pack or you're leading for others on behalf of others. If you're making decisions for yourself, that's a bit out of kilter for me. But as long as I'm keeping the people that I'm representing in my mind at all times during those decision-making processes, that's what I think really enables me to step up and feel confident in the person that I am and what I have to say. Cos I know, probably in younger years, I was terrified of that platform because [I'd ask myself] 'What if I say something wrong? How do I know that's what they want me to say?'* **Arizona Leger**

The future of work is real for Arizona. She's 24, passionate about serving her village and her people and super switched on. I admire Arizona's generation and their ability to call things out in such an articulate way. I've seen her on mainstream morning TV giving the hosts and panelists a run for their money. She is always authentic and advocating for the village through the mana (influence) she holds when speaking through various platforms. She always ensures her message is heard. It's inspiring to see **Arizona** empowered to take her space as a young Māori Pasifika leader who is owning her unique leadership potential.

Starting well

You too have the opportunity to own your own space by doing your research, finding organisations, boards, communities or charities, that have like-minded values to yours. As your values are important to you, the organisation you choose to align yourself with should demonstrate commitment to their values.

One of my many practices, for over a decade now, has been to always check the diversity of a new client's board and leadership team. Having no women on the board is a big NO GO space for me. Believe me, I've been there, I've done that, and it was 10 times the work and energy and 10 times less money and appreciation. What is your NO GO space?

I recommend going one extra step.
Via LinkedIn, find a connection in your network that works in or knows someone in the organisation or board you are targeting. Find out how the women in leadership roles operate. Are they known as advocates of other women? Outside of work how do they champion women? What's their track record for driving diversity in the organisation? Do they mentor, coach or volunteer for charities you would volunteer for? By doing this extra step you will be more aware of how women and diversity are prioritised in this new space.

Ann Francke, Co-Chair of UK's 30% Club, the organisation responsible for getting 30 percent of women on UK boards, adds her top tips.:

> *So if you are a woman and you are looking for a senior role in your sector, you can find out about the percentage of women in C-suite roles (short for chief roles, like chief executive, chief of staff, chief financial officer etc) or roles below the C-suite in your company, and other companies in that sector. And if your company is really bad at that, go to a company in your sector that's good. And don't [...] become victims or trapped [by] flexible working arrangements. [I think some women] think, 'Oh, I have to stay with company X because they let me work part-time or because they let me work flexibly around the needs of my childcare.'*
>
> *Don't assume that company Y won't do that. When you go in and you talk to company Y, [they may have] more women in senior positions, so [there may be] more [chance] of your own progression and a better culture. Just say to them, 'By the way, I have these flexible working arrangements and of course I'm assuming I can keep those.' Very enlightened employers will say, 'What are your flexible working arrangements? Yes, of course we'll honour those.'* **Ann Francke**

The lesson from Ann is to **take your space** and **ask for what you want**.

In meetings and on boards **Traci Houpapa** sets up her spaces in the following way:

> *As the Chairman in meetings I'm really clear about making space for everyone to have their say. I also make sure that I'm well briefed and I know what I'm talking so my comments and participation is clear, crisp and concise, and adds value to the discussions at the table. This approach puts everyone on notice that we're here to bring our best to the meetings; we're very clear about what we need to discuss and decide, and we get to the point.* **Traci Houpapa**

She insists on being well briefed, and also briefs herself through checklists, and has a list of what she wants to query in meetings – great practical, savvy ways for women of all ages to get into the doing.

Entry strategy

Spending time at the beginning of a new job learning the organisational culture and how they work , or with a new client or contract, is important. Establishing Kotahitanga or unity at the outset of a new job or contract creates a way of working together in spaces which are more empowering and transparent for all.

In Kotahitanga, all parties can have a voice and be heard in order to gain clarity of what is expected and, just as important, what is not acceptable behaviour. For example, mutual understanding of what respect means to all parties will avoid future misunderstandings. Everyone will have a different understanding of the word 'respect' and how it manifests.

People call it a 30, 60, 90 day plan. During your first 90 days in the organisation you should have a clear induction plan, onboarding process and a buddy in place to show you around and introduce you to key players. It is your job to take all the information they give you and translate it into a plan that your new line manager will buy into. By adopting this proactive approach, you are demonstrating you have a plan and are organised; that you can take the initiative and you are goal orientated.

I RECOMMEND A FEW STANDARD THINGS IN THE FIRST 90 DAY PLAN:
- Meet as many people outside of your immediate department as possible.
- Listen to and share your perspectives on the role, contract or project.
- Keep your plan broad at the beginning, break it down into Day 0–14, 14–30, 30–60 and 60–90
- Setup review meetings at the end of 30, 60 and 90 days and present back at 90 days your key learnings, achievements, and observations.
- Go the extra mile and have a quick 'feed-forward' form for others to complete, keep a record of your new colleagues' feed-forward of what has worked well in the past and more importantly what hasn't worked.

Remember you never get this induction time back again so use it wisely to set yourself up for success.

I guarantee, if you spend time at the beginning learning everyone's collective understanding of words like respect, trust, accountability, challenge, responsibility, confidentiality, safe, judgement-free, and tikanga (influencing cultural practices and protocols) you will have more honest, courageous conversations in the future.

Once you are in your chosen space of work, community or business, make sure you take ownership by taking care of the fundamentals.

1. **First and foremost, do the work you were hired to do**
2. **Ask for feedback on how you are doing**
3. **Build strong internal and external relationships and reciprocate**

By having the fundamentals in place, you can create, use, and take up your own space within the organisation.

How you set up your work, business, and career is critical to your future success, so do the work at the beginning. Now choose one thing you can do easily and effortlessly today and action it!

Exit strategy

You don't have to settle for anything less than what you want. If you are in an organisation that doesn't appreciate/respect your worth, then you don't need to stay. You can choose to leave their space on your own terms.

It's never too early to begin planning your exit strategy. In my experience, the main reason women are not leaving organisations on their own terms is they have not planned forward, or paid enough attention to the succession of their role so they are free to be promoted or move on. So, start the planning early. Bring someone you trust on board, find a mentor or invest in a coach. Exit strategies are not always because you are unhappy in your career or job space. You could be super successful and ready to move on.

Here are a few fundamental things to think about:

1. **Always keep your CV or resume up to date**
2. **Plan and have a timeframe to work towards exiting**
3. **Download all your relevant files and contacts before you hand in your notice**
4. **Save a portion of your current salary in case there is a gap between roles**
5. **Leverage your networks or recruitment agencies to find the next best fit**
6. **Leave on a high, you never know when you might meet up with your ex-employer.**

You will have different reasons for moving up or out depending on where you are on your journey. You may be moving sideways to broaden your experience.

You might be reading this and saying, 'It was the organisation's fault not mine,' or, 'I had no choice but to leave'. In some cases that may have been the case. However, I would challenge you to reframe the situation and ask yourself, 'What role did I play in that situation? What did I not see? What have I learnt about myself? Where are my blind spots?' We all have them.

I've been there, in those times where I was blaming everyone else for my demise. In London, I got overlooked for the Head of Department role in HR and Resourcing. I was devastated when the new hire turned up. Everything she said, did or asked me to do I resisted. The bottom line was they were looking for someone with X years of experience and a broader HR generalist. My preference was not policy, business partnering or being a generalist. I was focused on the sexy future-focused stuff such as talent and leadership development, strategic workforce planning or building talent pipelines, organisational culture and change programmes. That role was obviously not right for me at that time, but I spent a lot of time stewing about the unfairness of the appointment instead of choosing the role that was right for me – even if that meant leaving.

Planning your exit when you are at the top of your game is both strategic and savvy. In Chapter One, Jo talks about your achievements log linked to outcomes and results. Take responsibility for your space and let others take care of theirs.

BUILD AND MAINTAIN YOUR TRIBE

One of my top three values is making connections, both personally and professionally. I've never been one to shy away from that 'networking' word. It's a form of connection to a tribe of like-minded people and I'm genuinely curious about other people's journeys and stories.

A great example of building a tribe of like-minded women is the UK's 30% Club. One of the things they do well, amongst many, is work on normalising the presence of three or more women at the board/executive/senior leadership table. As we know there is power in numbers. The reality is, often women are the lone one or two voices.

The thing that we always say and the reason that we have the 30% Club is that if you're one out of 10 in the room, everything you say, every time you open your mouth, is seen as the 'female voice' and it's hard. When you're two people in the room everyone confuses you. Even if you're completely different – you're from different countries, you look different – they'll mix your names up because you're those two things we call women.

That still happens to me from time to time in meetings […] when there aren't enough of us. Once you get to three then you're normalised and you can start to be heard a bit more. It is very hard if you're the lone woman. But one of the things I've learned from watching others, (and it's worked for me), is choosing some people in advance to discuss the point that you want to make and being a bit savvy about getting their support in the meeting.[Choose] some board members, or the group members in a meeting that you get on with and you trust, and get [...] them onside before the meeting. [Ensure] that they're going to support you so that you [can] make your point. Then if someone doesn't listen to it or ignores it, or whatever, they're going to stand out. **Brenda Trenowden**

I also think Brenda's advice applies to younger women and girls. Find your allies in a group or team situation and if you can find a male to add to the mix even better.

Brenda goes on to share how she supported **Ann Francke**, a senior, well-respected, international businesswoman, to be heard. The outcome was a win–win for both.

It was an open discussion and there was someone chairing, and they had said, 'Ann, could you speak about x'. Ann started speaking and another man cut her off and just started speaking about something else [...] and no one said a word. It was so rude, it was incredible, and everyone just kind of let that happen.

So when he finished speaking, I put my hand up and the chair said, 'Yes, Brenda, what would you like to add?' And I said, 'Well, actually, I thought what Ann was talking about was really interesting and I just wonder if she could continue that point because I'd like to hear more about it.' I didn't know Ann before that evening, but we became friends as a result. Roll forward a few years and she has just taken over from me as Global Chair of the 30% Club. **Brenda Trenowden**

Ann eventually became the Co-Chair of the 30% Club and this dynamic duo continue to break the glass ceiling and exceed the milestones they set for women on boards and C-suite roles in the UK. Bravo ladies!

But what if you are not corporate? You may be thinking, 'Does this still apply to me?'

Yes, yes, yes. *Tribe* is the keyword here. Everyone wants to belong to a tribe. We are hard-wired to belong, regardless of culture, sexual orientation, diversity, ethnicity, religion, life experience, education or race. Women are on the lookout for tribes, organisations, boards, groups and communities that meet our social, personal, professional, economic and human needs. Whatever that is for each of us will be different, such as belonging to women's networks, community groups, not-for-profits, social enterprises, coffee and book clubs. Michelle Obama created a global tribe of young women hungry for education. Sheryl Sandberg, the author of *Lean In*, created her tribe of corporate women who continue to lean in and influence leadership globally. Who are your tribe?

Take your physical space

We've covered a lot, in terms of finding your space, your entry and exit strategy and growing your tribe. Now you need to take your physical space. Position yourself *physically* to take your space in meetings and around the board table.

Did you know women have been taught to sit with legs crossed taking up less space, while men sprawl? FYI, according to the Oxford online dictionary, 'manspreading' describes 'the practice whereby a man adopts a sitting position with his legs wide apart, in such a way as to encroach on an adjacent seat'. It is a behaviour that is commonly spotted on public transport. NYC ran a campaign against manspreading with a graphic to go alongside it.

The point is that you can choose to physically and strategically position yourself and it can be the difference between being heard or not.

Note who strategically takes the head of a table in your next meeting. I will always give myself a few seconds to scan the seating of a meeting before I take my seat, even when I go to dinner. I'm careful to sit in a position where I can see what's going on from multiple angles.

AMY CUDDY   Photo: Evgenia Eliseeva

Make sure to watch Amy Cuddy's TED Talk, *Your Body Language May Shape Who You Are*.[11] Jo and I use the power pose in the mirror before keynote speeches or important meetings where we are presenting. Whether you believe in Amy's study or not it helps to understand that adopting expansive postures can cause people to feel more powerful. She answers her critics here. She answers her academic critics in new research published in Psychological Science.

Ask for feed-forward in order to improve

When you think about some of the feedback you have received in the past has it moved you forward or back? Feed-forward does exactly what it says on the tin – it moves you forward in order for you to take your space.

MAN SPREADING

Brené Brown, the world-renowned researcher on vulnerability and shame turned celebrity author says, 'if you are not in the arena and getting your arse kicked, then I am not interested in your feedback'. I highly recommend Brené's newest Netflix film, *The Call To Courage*.[12]

BRENÉ BROWN   Photo: WIKIPEDIA

In my experience as a leader, working with thousands of women around the world, being open to receiving feed-forward versus feedback is the difference between good and great leadership. Feed-forward is future focused and supports a way forward. It is a skill that is largely under-utilised and under-valued as a resource for self-growth, and self-development. Even if the feed-forward is poorly wrapped, look for the taonga (treasure) in what is underneath the words. Some of my best feed-forwards has been some of the harshest.

One of my mantras, adopted from my business partner Jeanine Bailey, is: 'there is no such thing as failure. There is only feed-forward and learning'. When I'm failing I know I am learning and in my experience the more spectacular the fall, the bigger the learning.

As women, we can be our own harshest inner critic. We all have an individual and collective responsibility to reframe the narrative that goes on within. You know, the narrative that is on constant replay. One of my mentors drummed into me that you are what you focus on, so focus on the 80 percent value you bring and outsource the other 20 percent to experts.

Creating spaces for more women

I often say to other women that we can all be leaders in our unique spaces. What I actually mean is that there is so much work to do there is space for all of us. Whatever your passion, to support women is to start creating spaces for women to step into. You can see by reading the first two chapters that it is a collective effort that will create the global change we need to see.

To make sure you are heard, try these practical tips:

- **Get to your headline message quickly and then follow up with the detail; avoid justifying your message; say what you mean**
- **Stick to the point of the discussion, avoid going off-topic and guide everyone back to the topic at hand; be assertive.**

Volunteering in spaces you are passionate about is so rewarding. For the last five years I have worked with young 14–17-year-old Māori and Pacific women of Otara in South Auckland, New Zealand. It fills me up to know that as a voluntary committee or tribe of like-minded humans we are making a difference in our very small way.

We all have a responsibility to support each other to **take our space**. If you don't who will?

Role modelling how you take your space, is as important for other women to see as it is for you to coach and mentor the next woman. When we step forward we give other women permission to step forward too. This includes advocacy, sponsorship, succession and being the hand up to create a space for the next leader, manager, graduate and board member.

Too often women who get to a certain position in life forget to look left and look right to see who is at the table. Always ask yourself, who is not at this table with me today? I guarantee you'll think of one or two women who would make a difference. Then be bold and ask that same question of those around the table.

Simply by speaking up for another woman – about who would be the best fit for a new job in your organisation, or as a director on your board – is taking your space.

Women should never underestimate the power we hold, when in key decision-making roles, to advocate for policy changes that can impact women's inclusion, leadership, diversity and equity. There are many examples in this book of women creating transformational change for young girls and women.

What you implement may not make an impact today, but the goal is to be both outcomes focused and output driven. You need to ensure you can measure delivery and still have an eye on the bigger aspirations, vision and future success. What can you do today?

Amplification and alignment of what is important to you or your organisation is a great way to support social justice issues that you are passionate about. If you know you can support other women by lending your voice to a platform that works for you too, go for it.

Influencing others, as women in corporations, communities, boards and business, is essential to young girls still finding their voices and owning their space. For gender equality and equity to become a reality we must all step forward, one woman at a time. Just as all 14 fabulous women in our book have done.

How To Checklist - Take your space

- **Find your unique space and own it.** If you are not sure, survey, email, or call a group of your trusted networks of friends, family and colleagues and ask them these three questions: what three words would you use to describe me? What do you believe are my strengths? What would you like me to do more of?

- **Say what you mean.** Get used to saying what you want to say, not what you think people want you to say. Your words are powerful. Once you decide how you want to say it, state it upfront and then follow up with the detail.

- **Find early adopters.** When you are challenging social norms start with those who believe in what you believe in.

- **Journal and write more.** The more you physically write down your dreams, aspirations and goals the more you activate the neuro pathways in your brain that focus on achieving your goals. Journaling, keeping diaries, and writing consistently every day will support you to activate your success. Try writing down the same achievable goal every day for 30 days. All the gurus swear by it.

- **Define your success.** You can do this self-reflection work for yourself or with a coach, mentor or froach (friend/coach) to help you define what success is for you. Ask yourself what would your life, career, or business be like if everything was exactly as it was meant to be? What would you be seeing? What would you be saying to yourself? What would others be saying to you? What would you be feeling?

- **Amplify other women's messages.** Align with like-minded women, test and try out tribes that have shared values, share other women's content via your website, social media platforms or via email.

- **Attract your tribe.** Start telling your story from your unique space. Play to your strengths. If writing is what you do well, then write. If verbal communication or video is your preferred platform then do that. Share what is important to you and use the feedback that you have received to validate what you share. Be consistent, share one email or one Facebook post every Monday. Build from there.

- **Have a 30, 60, 90 day plan.** Start with one goal for week one, month one, month two and month three. Then build from there. When you are starting something new, or moving into a new space, it requires some sort of plan. Even if you don't stick to the plan it is important you have an idea of what it looks like.

- **Get comfortable with your physical presence.** Trial and test how you turn up in meetings, how you introduce topics that are important to you, and remember to enroll others to back you up. Try opening a window on entering a room, to acknowledge your presence.

- **Invest in support.** Get a mentor, expert, coach, trainer, teacher; whatever it takes to support you creating your unique space for self-empowerment. And then turn around and offer to support other women.

- **Finally, trust and believe in yourself.** Even when you're wrong, you're right because you will have learnt something that will move you forward.

Endnotes

1   https://aucklanduniversitypress.co.nz/dancing-with-the-king-the-rise-and-fall-of-the-king-country-1864-1885/

2   https://womendeliver.org/2018/womans-place-politics/

3   https://www.glamour.com/story/michelle-obama-new-education-initiative-global-girls-alliance

4   https://economictimes.indiatimes.com/news/economy/policy/structural-to-sectoral-reforms-agenda-for-team-modi-2-0/articleshow/69590869.cms

5   https://www.minister.defence.gov.au/minister/lreynolds

6   https://www.ipu.org/news/press-releases/2019-03/one-in-five-ministers-woman-according-new-ipuun-women-map

7   https://www.ipu.org/resources/publications/reports/2020-03/women-in-parliament-1995-2020-25-years-in-review

8   https://books.google.co.nz/books?id=vyU_DwAQBAJ&printsec=frontcover#v=onepage&q&f=false

9   https://www.stuff.co.nz/national/101677420/equal-pay-champion-kristine-bartlett-named-2018-new-zealander-of-the-year

10 https://malechampionsofchange.com/wp-content/uploads/2019/12/2019-MCC-Impact-Report_Summary_FINAL-1.pdf

11 TED Talk, *Your Body Language May Shape Who You Are* link: https://journals.sagepub.com/eprint/CzbNAn7Ch677irK9yMGH/full

12 https://nzhistory.govt.nz/people/meri-te-tai-mangakahia

LIFT OFF

– Jo Cribb –

* **Work out your why**
* **Make a plan to get ahead**
* **Take small steps frequently**
* **Don't give up**
* **How to promote yourself**

Ever cringed when someone read out your bio: the 200 words that describe the last decade of your career? It usually sounds so planned and logical, when really it's been a mixture of scary, frustrating, exhilarating, confusing, boring, and the mundane.

What also doesn't factor into my bio are the hundreds of cover letters drafted and job application forms filled in, the many interviews and the 'thanks, but no thanks' emails I have received. You don't hear about the times I've cried over not getting a job I wanted.

Yes, my career trajectory makes sense in the rear view mirror, and I did have an idea where I was heading, but the journey has been far from clear or easy. Nor is it over; I feel like I am just warming up.

For me, I wanted to choose a path that suited me, that of a credible leader, celebrating that I am also a mother; I wanted to stay true to my style of getting things done (which has never involved raising my voice or thumping my fists on the table) and true to my values, such as serving others. But it is only in retrospect that I can see this.

There were some women leaders I admired because they were authentic. One stopped me in a corridor when I was a junior and said I should aspire to be a chief executive (CE). While I shrugged it off at the time, her comment stayed with me as a confidence boost that just kept giving. Fifteen years later, when my appointment as CE was announced, she was one of the first to congratulate me, reminding me how important women can be in encouraging other women.

I know my experience of navigating the career minefield is shared by many of us, whether we are employees, self-employed, or in unpaid work, and regardless of the type of organisation we work within.

You are not alone

Actually, that is not quite true. If you are on a board or in a CE position you are more likely to be alone. A 2019 review of 23,000 leadership roles in 350 of the largest companies in the UK found that, if you are a woman, you are less likely to be promoted into a leadership role than a man[1]. Less than 30 percent of senior leadership positions are held by women, and most of these are in HR (over 60 percent) and general counsel roles (approximately 30 percent). We certainly do not get to put our hands on the money (15 percent of financial directors are women).

"Describe what you can bring to this company."

The New Yorker Cartoonist, Will McPhail

Women aren't usually the CE either.[2] There were twice as many FTSE 100 chief executives or chairs called John than women in those jobs. The same was true in New Zealand in 2019, when only five women led a stock exchange listed company – but there were eight Marks.[3]

Women now make up 30 percent of seats on UK corporates, but there are still boards with no women and others with a 'one and done' approach. The rate is only 22 percent in New Zealand and progress is slow.[4] Eighteen percent of the New Zealand boards of listed companies have no women members.

In her book, *Create a Gender-balanced Workplace*, Ann Francke found that men were 40 percent more likely to get promoted than women. She blames it on the 'Paula Principle'. This is a variation of the 'Peter Principle' that you may have already heard of, where people are promoted to one level above their competence. The Paula Principle is the opposite. Women are likely to be promoted to one level *below* their competence.[5]

For those of us who own businesses or are self-employed, to grow our business we will face barriers. A 2018 study found just nine percent of funding for UK start-ups is awarded to women-led businesses annually and men are 86 percent more likely to be funded by venture capital.[6]

So why aren't we being promoted, appointed to boards, or backed in our business ventures?

THERE ARE MANY REASONS.

Women tend to do more housework than their male partners, irrespective of their age, income, or own workloads.[7] According to the OECD in 2016, Australian women spent 168 minutes doing housework every day, while their male partners spent 93 minutes per day. British men did the least (66 minutes per day).[8] Women also took on the bulk of the childcare and were 10 times more likely to stay at home with a sick child than their male partner was.[9] Women were also most likely to take responsibility for caring for elderly relatives.

AVERAGE MINUTES PER DAY SPENT ON ROUTINE HOUSEWORK BY GENDER, IN OECD COUNTRIES PLUS CHINA, INDIA AND SOUTH AFRICA, AS OF 2016

A study in 2019 (and updated in 2020) found 63 percent of New Zealand women's work is unpaid, compared with 35 percent of men's.[10] In 2015 women in paid work and caring for children clocked up far more hours a week than the average CEO.[11]

Not only do we often take a substantial career hit when we take parental leave (and parental leave in most countries is taken primarily by women),[12] our other responsibilities mean it is not surprising that many women seek reduced paid hours or prioritise flexibility over promotion.

The support structures we need to fast track our careers (or just keep them on track) while caring for young children or elderly relatives aren't available to many of us, such as flexible hours, options to work from home, and the ability to take career breaks without being penalised and side-lined.

Then when we actually make it to work (after cleaning up the bottle of milk that spilt in the fridge and the baby spit off our shirts) we face a range of biases about how we are viewed as workers and leaders. We will be expected to prove that we are competent by constantly demonstrating that we are. We will have to walk a tightrope of expected behaviour; needing to be seen as having 'male' traits to be a real leader, but if we demonstrate these, we can be regarded as too aggressive and not feminine enough. Then, if we have children, we may hit the 'maternal wall'; whatever we choose will be wrong (stay at home, work part-time, work full-time).[13] We might be over-mentored (because we are seen to need to be fixed or improved) or under-sponsored (the doors aren't opened for us by other men or women).[14] But if we work hard and play the game, we might get to be the 'one and done': the woman promoted to show that your organisation has gender equality.

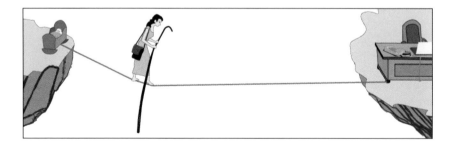

However, most of us won't even get close to the ladder. New research by McKinsey, of over 60, 000 Canadian and American employees, shows that there is a missing rung: the first one. Many of us don't ever get that first management role.[15]

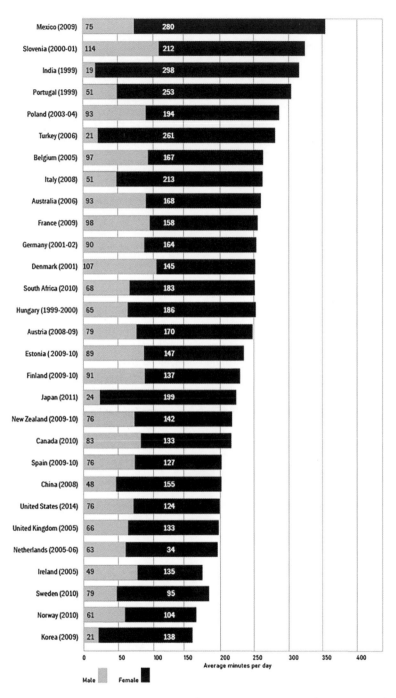

Average minutes per day spent on routine housework by gender, in OECD countries plus China, India and South Africa, as of 2016

So again it's not surprising that many women respond with what Ann Francke calls 'the tiara syndrome'. We put our heads down and work hard, hoping that someone will come along, recognise us and promote us.

But hope is not the best strategy for getting promoted.

> *You get the break because you're doing something and somebody somewhere recognises this – but you need both. You have to have done the mahi [work] and then you need the person who sees it and gives you the opportunity.*
> **Anjum Rahman**

Or worse, we pit ourselves against each other. Sheryl Sandberg talks about this in *Lean In*. 'Queen Bee' is the term she uses to describe women in senior leadership roles who use their position to keep other women (worker bees) down. The Queen Bee may behave like this for self-preservation, for the need to feel worthy, or maybe she is being rewarded for maintaining the status quo. I call these women 'rope cutters', they turn and push the ladder away, or cut the rope so no other women can follow them.

> *We already have a lot of senior women judges and law partners. But the problem is not every [woman who attains a powerful position has the willingness] or habit to support others. I have experienced more hostile attitudes [in] my career in court from female women colleagues and judges than those from the males. I was not expecting that. I was naive to think the women who are senior and have become successful ahead of others would be more supportive, or empathetic. That was not always my experience. I [have] been put down for my ethnicity, my youthful appearance, or my boutique size firm. It is hard not to be affected by the institutional bias, but until the changes happen the feeling of powerlessness even when there are plenty of women on top already is a constant battle.*
> **Royal Reed**

We may choose to be liked rather than promoted. We may decide that the BS in organisations is too much and not worth our energy. Or we may be exhausted, just trying to get to the starting line each day.

Here's what you can do
Okay, so let's get noticed, promoted, appointed, funded, and invested in.

WORK OUT YOUR 'WHY'
It took me a long time to figure this out. I guess I was always trying to 'do the right thing' because I assumed it was the way to get ahead. In primary school, we were taught to be well behaved, to put your hand up and wait to be asked, and to do what was expected of good girls: study, read, and do as we were told. Sitting up straight in the front row, however, didn't work for adult me. So I worked out what I really cared about and how I wanted to spend my time; I steered towards this and haven't looked back.

Traci Houpapa talks about finding something that makes your heart sing, **Linda Jenkinson** refers to it as finding *her* formula; **Bridget Foliaki-Davis** sees her cooking as a vocation not a job; and **Jackie Clark** is all about the importance of finding joy in your work. She warns that trying to fit in and follow the line, like the girls in the front row angling to be teacher's pet, is not an effective strategy for success in adult life.

> *White, middle-class women are the fraidiest of the fraidiest. I see them and I go, why [...] would you want to live as a cookie cutter for the rest of your life? It's so miserable [...] not standing out. Stand the fuck out. [...] I can be brave about that now, but [...] I've always fought to be allowed to be who I am. For my husband, I was too much or not enough. Fuck them. Fuck them all. You are who you are.* **Jackie Clarke**

Linda reminds us that we have already have the basic ingredients to make our lives as we wish, we just need to decide what we want:

> *Basically, decide that you actually have everything you need to have life as you want it. Then look and you'll start noticing all these things that are [...] there to help you, that you didn't notice before. When you are pregnant you notice every pregnant woman, right? By taking that perspective, you suddenly see all this opportunity that's right there for you, by focusing your mind.* **Linda Jenkinson**

There are effective activities you can do to help you define what you care about:
- Visualise yourself as an old woman talking with your grandchildren. What would you want to tell them about your life? I guarantee you won't focus on telling them the towels in your laundry cupboard were always neatly folded. Morbid as it sounds, writing your obituary now as you would like it to be will focus you on what matters to you.

- Ask a close friend what are the five characteristics they most identify with you. Then reflect on whether these are what you want to be known for. A good friend of mine wrote himself a tag line – a short sentence that defines who he is. Another friend has an image that captures the colours and feelings that matter most to her. She uses it regularly to refocus her energies.

All the women we interviewed have defined their *why*, in their own way. They've worked out what they want, and some could say they have been shameless in working towards it.

DON'T PUT IT OFF
How many times have you heard a friend say, 'I will do that when I have lost weight/ saved money/ stopped smoking/ gone to the gym more'? We tend to put off something important until our world is perfect. Or we put off something important until someone else's world is perfect: until my husband has a better job/ the kids are more settled at school/ the cat isn't sick... My unrequested fortieth birthday present of late-stage cancer certainly taught me that there will never be a perfect time – the perfect time is right now.

We all know this. We get constant reminders: we lose loved ones, there are disasters, accidents, we see other people's grief, and the 'seize the day' memes flash up in our FB and Insta posts all the time. And yet we still wait; we put off the things that are most important to us.

Alexia Hilbertidou believes this is especially true for younger women who are often expected to wait until they are more experienced, but as she points out:

> *You're never too young to create change, to get out there into your community and make a difference. The best time to start is now. You have everything within you, right now, to be a positive force for good.* **Alexia Hilbertidou**

MAKE A PLAN AND DO THE WORK

So you have decided what you want. Now make a plan and take off. For Alexia this meant planning three actions she could do now. It could be updating your LinkedIn page, inviting someone to coffee, or going to a networking event.

You are most powerful when you are running towards something, rather than trying to run away from something, Brenda Trenowden advises. Don't leave a bad job, instead start a great one. But, as Royal's experience has shown, don't be naïve about discrimination and those who may not wish you to succeed. Include barriers and strategies to overcome them in your plan.

TAKE BABY STEPS EVERY DAY

I find this way of planning works for me; breaking it into manageable short sprints, rather than a plan that's too long, which can be overwhelming. I set four goals each year, under the areas of finance, something to learn or develop, one thing I want to achieve, and a personal goal around health, fitness or family. This keeps me balanced and stretches me, while being practical enough to keep me focused.

Bridget Foliaki-Davis also works on the basis of incremental improvements as the basis of her success.

> *I always see every episode of my life as a learning opportunity. You can just keep doing the same thing and getting the same results, but I've always wanted to get better results, even if it's just a millimetre of an improvement. For me, improvements don't have to be tenfold. They can literally be just the tiniest little steps, but you're always moving forward.*
>
> *I don't know if I was born with that; maybe it's the kitchen environment where we're always looking to make a dish a little bit better; be brought to the customer a little bit faster. It's those small changes that count.* **Bridget Foliaki-Davis**

The beauty of taking small steps is that if it happens to be the wrong one or not quite right yet, it is only a small step and is easy to retrace your path. The management gurus and tech heads call this 'failing fast'. There is something to this approach. It is not about waiting for perfection, endlessly refining your skills until you are 'good enough', it is about taking a step forward, and then another one. You have very little to lose after just one step.

PROMOTE YOURSELF

You will need help with your plan – a network of supporters who believe in you and your work; your allies. **Royal Reed** says she's been very planned in creating a network for herself.

> *I sought help. I even pay, now that I can, for senior legal mentors, mostly men, to help me. What I have found, which is sad, is that buying time with senior people works.* **Royal Reed**

The importance of mentors, sponsors, allies, networks – other people who will help you succeed – cannot be overstated. Often, however, we are too busy doing the work and not taking time to build our team around us.

> *Women typically don't spend enough time thinking about sponsorship and stakeholder management … [They] just work hard to do a good job - but don't do any of the extra bits around it in terms of building those sponsors who will really help stick their neck out for them; [who will] use their political capital for them and push them forward.* **Brenda Trenowden**

Promoting yourself can feel conflicting, for some cultures. For Samoans, traditionally someone else would introduce you. In Māoridom, you introduce yourself through your 'pepeha', which links you with your mountain, river, sea and land. It is your ancestral lineage first; your name is the most irrelevant part of your introduction and comes last – the collective before the individual.

Rachel's coaching clients often say, 'I'm not good at promoting myself, it doesn't feel natural' or, 'it's not our way to talk about ourselves.' Being Māori, she totally understands that collective mindset. There is a proverb in Māori culture that says, the kumara [sweet potato] doesn't speak of its sweetness. Her interpretation, and there are many, is that as leaders we should be humble. She argues that we need to collectively role model what this looks like, in a way that works for you, your culture, and your why.

Remember you are so much more than your job title. As **Stacey** says, 'Your life isn't your title – your work isn't who you are, it's what you do.'

> *When you are part of a culture that yearns for connection, then that will come out in many different forms. I believe we struggle sometimes in individual settings and knowing that a lot of the world is structured for the individual, but our whakapapa*

[history], our DNA, asks us to connect and pushes us to connect always and be part of a collective.

I don't have titles that say I'm a leader so much. What I do is look to see what I can offer. What is something that I can do that hadn't existed before? **Stacey Morrison**

A mentor is someone you go to for advice. Often they are someone you trust who isn't your direct manager. They should care about you and provide support for your career and personal development. Mentoring relationships come in all shapes and sizes, formal, informal, planned or one-off. The best way to find an excellent mentor is to think about the areas you need help in and find someone you respect. Most people will be flattered if you ask them for advice.

A coach is someone you usually pay, and a session can cost more than a day's wages. Your coach should act just like the coach of a sports team, trying to help you win the next game or finish the season ahead. Coaching relationships usually last for a fixed period with a specific aim – like helping you to get your next role.

A sponsor is someone who believes in your abilities and aims to help you succeed; they are prepared to help you. Often, they do this by introducing you to people or saying great things about you. They may even put their reputation on the line for you. We all could do with some of these and, like Brenda says, sometimes we all need another woman with her hand in the small of your back pushing you forward and encouraging you to take that next step.

Brenda suggests we need to sit down and map out who we need in our team to get ahead and then get their help:

If you're a mid-level career woman now, you need to focus on sponsorship and stakeholder management.

Everyone I mentor I've talked to about it and said, 'Look, have you sat down and looked at your organisation and [the] path between you and the CEO? Do you really understand it? Do you know who the key influencers and decision-makers are? Who are the people that will have a say over your career and the roles that you want to do?'

Sit down and work out a stakeholder map and find some mentors, but also find some sponsors in the organisation. Have people that are going to help you get to the position you need to get to and figure out a way that you can build a relationship that's beneficial to them and to you. **Brenda Trenowden**

NIP NEGATIVE IN THE BUD

Negative thoughts are likely to enter your mind. 'What if I fail? What if they don't like me? I don't think I can do this. I don't deserve a promotion.' In their book *The Confidence Code*, Katty Kay and Claire Shipman call these annoying ear worms 'negative automatic thoughts'. Like a cheesy pop song, they stick in our heads on high repeat.

They recommend that we acknowledge that the thoughts are there and that most of us have them, even extremely successful high profile women. They suggest writing them down each time you think of a negative thought. Many of these thoughts pop up as we go to sleep or (worse) if we wake up in the middle of the night.

To get rid of them, go looking for the counterpoint of view for each negative thought. 'What if I fail? What if I succeed? What if they don't like me? What if they end up respecting me?' By doing this we are refocusing and controlling our thoughts. Over time, we will grow stronger mental muscles that mean we end up hearing less of them and getting rid of any that do slip in, faster.

DON'T GIVE UP

Nothing goes to plan, and sometimes that is great. New opportunities present themselves and we can rework our plans to be even better. Sometimes it isn't so great.

But it's when it is going bad that real success can happen. This is when we build resilience, or in Brenda's word, our rhino skins:

Having come from financial services, [which is] an incredibly male dominated industry, I've said to women over the years, 'If you want to do this you've really got to find inner strength and you've got to grow that rhinoceros skin and toughen up.'

[There have] been tough battles for the women who've made great progress for us over the years. It's figuring out how to find strength and resilience. I have a very rare form of cancer and it's an ongoing battle. [But] it doesn't have to be cancer – it can just be working in a difficult industry or juggling young children and/or aged parents and work. One of the big things that women need to work on [is] understanding what are the things that help fuel you and what gives you that resilience and strength? Because resilience isn't about just being strong and powering through – it's about having the ability to bounce back when you've had a knock. I think so many women feel they have to keep powering through until they fall over [...] They don't allow themselves the opportunity to refuel, and re-energise, and be resilient. We could learn a lot from elite athletes – they build in recovery time so that they can achieve peak performance. **Brenda Trenowden**

Here's how we can help each other

One of the most important things we can do is to help each other. If you are able to send the elevator down, do so, so other women can rise. Use all the levers that you have to support others. In my career so far, it hasn't been what I have achieved in deliverables that has been the most satisfying, it has been watching those who I have sponsored succeed.

If you have any niggling thoughts about your success being compromised by the success of other women, remember that the sky is more than big enough for all of us to be stars and the world needs us all to be shining brilliantly.

Let's start with small actions. Let's talk well of each other for a start. We can all do this.

> One woman head-hunter [who] was looking for a CEO of a company told me, 'If I call women and say, "What do you think about this woman?" the women will feel obliged to say, "Well, these are the things that maybe are her shortcomings and you might find that she's...blah blah blah... but here's the positive point..." They want to be balanced and objective and make sure that they're seen to give a really objective view.'
>
> Whereas, when she calls men about other men they'll go, 'Oh my God, he's brilliant – you should have hired him already. He's absolutely great for the job.' I think it's something in the way that we're socialised. Women don't want to be seen to be supporting other women. Well, the men have been doing that since time began.
> **Brenda Trenowden**

How To Checklist - Lift Off

- **Be clear about what you want for yourself.** Be clear about your 'why'. Ambition is not a swear word, i. It just means you want some things and you are working towards them. Be clear about your ambition for yourself.

- **Don't wait for your life to be perfect.** Start now.

- **Make a career plan for how you are going to get to where you want to be.** Start with one step forward, follow it with another.

- **Work out who you need to be on your supporters team.** Then go and get them on board.

- **Fight your negative thoughts.**

- **Speak well of other women.** They will then speak well of you.

Endnotes

1 https://ftsewomenleaders.com/wp-content/
uploads/2019/11/HA-Review-Report-2019.pdf

2 https://www.execpipeline.com/women-count-2019/

3 https://www.stuff.co.nz/business/117690424/gender-
gap-more-men-named-mark-running-companies-
than-women

4 https://www.nzherald.co.nz/business/news/article.
cfm?c_id=3&objectid=12196193

5 Francke, Ann (2019) Create a Gender-balanced
Workplace, Penguin Random House, UK

6 https://www.telegraph.co.uk/women/business/
women-entrepreneurs-opening-businesses-faster-
still-dont-receive/

7 https://www.sciencedaily.com/
releases/2017/09/170926105448.htm

8 https://www.statista.com/statistics/521919/time-
spent-housework-countries/

9 https://www.kff.org/womens-health-policy/issue-
brief/data-note-balancing-on-shaky-ground-women-
work-and-family-health/

10 https://women.govt.nz/work-skills/utilising-womens-
skills/paid-and-unpaid-work

11 https://www.stuff.co.nz/life-style/parenting/mums-
life/79847115/working-mothers-work-longer-hours-
than-the-average-ceo

12 https://women.govt.nz/sites/public_files/paper-
valuing-motherhood.pdf

13 Williams, Joan and Rachel Dempsey (2017) What
Works for Women in Work, New York University Press,
NY

14 https://www.researchgate.net/publication/46168700_
Why_men_still_get_more_promotions_than_women

15 https://leanin.org/women-in-the-workplace-2019

OWN YOUR CONFIDENCE

– Rachel Petero –

* Create your confidence cocktail
* Build your awareness and experience alternative world views
* Practice saying No. It is a full sentence
* Power pose as you stand in your mana and tell your story
* Face your fears, get uncomfortable and stop comparing
* Help others be confident

Over 15 years I set up home from scratch three times, in three completely different cultures and continents (UK, Middle East and back to Aotearoa). While making new friends, travelling and going to some of the best concerts of all time, I also started three new industry careers and launched a business; all amidst a global financial crisis.

Why do that to myself? One career change can be daunting enough, but three is next level. Each change involved a steep learning curve for the first six to nine months, and by month 12 there was a mix of relief, satisfaction, and safety. I had proven to my new employer, and to myself, that I could cut it.

Surprisingly, safety isn't a high value of mine. Freedom, whānau and financial well-being are.

Starting my first business was the total opposite of safety. It was all about risk. What risks was I willing to take? If you have ever done a risk profile with a financial advisor you will know that there are low, medium or high-risk profiles. I was once told I was off the top of the scale on risk. (I took that as a compliment.)

Business for me is like continually jumping from one mountain top to the next in slow motion. You're not too sure if you will make it or if you will fall into the valley below with a thump. When I started my first business in 2010 there was so much I didn't know. What I noticed was the more I jumped, the more I fell, and the more I learnt what not to do next time, so the more confidence I gained, and the more I trusted myself and others.

In those early days, I learnt that confidence is a muscle you must train. It starts with small internal shifts like mindfulness mantras, gratitude, affirmations and one-liners of simple daily self-talk rituals. It continues by constantly being around people who inspire, love and energise you.

This confidence recipe of affirming self-talk, saying yes to new challenges, running towards risk, and jumping through failure has impacted every part of my life, including my relationships, my health, my whānau my friends, and my business. One day, not sure when, confidence switched to self-confidence. It's like an internal knowing, telling you everything will be okay.

In the beginning, I saw my confidence as external, that 'fake it till you make it' approach. I realised that who I was being externally had aligned with who I was internally. As a result that inner voice became louder, more courageous, more fearless – more me.

My self-confidence muscle was continually at the 'gym' being fed the 'happy hormones' of dopamine and serotonin. It's addictive.

One of the biggest lessons I've learned as part of this journey is to trust myself. Even when I'm wrong, I'm right, because I've learnt something to use the next time that speed bump shows up on the road. The 'trust myself' muscle is another workout, and you may need to attend that class more than two or three times a day!

Having worked with over 150 cultures across three continents, in corporate and in community, I have learnt that that confidence can look quite different for ethnic, Indigenous, and women of colour. It comes in many shapes and forms. Confidence of cultural identity, connection to nature, spirituality and traditional knowledge, have all played a big part in my life.

In the Middle East, I met and worked with highly confident, modern, devout Muslim women. I often got into arguments with western expatriates who would generalise and say women in a hijab or abaya were suppressed and dominated by their husbands. (None of them had ever spoken to a Muslim woman, by the way.)

In some Pacific cultures (in Samoan culture for example), you traditionally would be introduced by another person, and it would be frowned upon to introduce yourself. Lowering your eyes shows respect, whereas in a western context this could be viewed as submissive, weak and lacking confidence.

In Māori culture, we don't introduce ourselves as an individual. Instead we introduce our ancestors, our environment, our tribal area, our turangawaewae, our standing place (from where we stand and for me where I will eventually lay to rest), our canoe that bought us across the Pacific to Aotearoa, our parents, and lastly our name.

The point is, there are many worldviews of what confidence is and isn't. Whatever it is for you, make sure you own it, work it and grow it.

What does the evidence tell us?

There are over 1,200 book results on amazon.com when you type in 'women' and 'confidence'. The two best-selling books are Brené Brown's *The Gifts of Imperfection* and *Daring Greatly*.[1]

Clearly we haven't quite mastered this confidence thing but there is much guidance already available for you. That's why Jo and I didn't want to write another book about it. Confidence is only one of the ingredients you will need to **Take Your Space.**

The research I've read is not as black and white as I first thought, but here are the things I believe are important for you to know as we go through this chapter:

On one hand, the evidence is focused largely on external factors which demonstrate confidence through the physical way you dress, project your voice, take action, cross or don't cross your legs, use direct eye contact, lean in, and so on. Basically saying, no matter how we feel internally or externally, you can fake confidence or 'fake it, till you make it' – that 1970s cliché phrase.[2]

The flip side is how women manage self-confidence internally. Internal factors, or the emotive side, is a deep topic of science, neurology and belief systems and to cover it well would take another three books. The subject includes, but is not limited to, how you feel about yourself, your behaviours, beliefs, values, self-talk, self-value, self-development, self-discovery, self-growth, self-reflection, self-awareness, self-improvement, and self-help.

You get the point. When you are able to align the external and internal factors of confidence you are on the pathway to self-mastery.

Warning, before you proceed, there is no magic confidence-wand to take you from zero to 100 overnight. You have to do the internal work, dig deep and ask yourself, 'Where does my lack of confidence come from?' Imagine your confidence (both internal and external) was a car driving down the highway. Things are going well; you have everything under

HOW YOU FEEL ABOUT YOURSELF

self-development self-growth self-improvement
self-discovery self-awareness self-help

What you believe

What your self-talk is saying

How you feel about yourself

How you value yourself

How you behave

Your core values

SEA OF SELF-DOUBT

control. But then you hit a roadblock – even worse, you hit an invisible roadblock. In the next few pages, we will tackle some of those blocks, obvious or hidden. To achieve your full potential and live life with confidence, we need to shine the light on our invisible roadblocks in order to breakthrough these limiting beliefs. Let this chapter be that confidence breakthrough for you.

What are the roadblocks?
SOCIAL MEDIA, THE DARK SIDE

Technology and social media can change lives for good for young girls and women. Technology is a lifeline to social acceptance, social consciousness, social connectedness, democratising information, growing e-commerce businesses, growing your personal brand, and confidence online. But the dark side of this story is disturbing. Data shows that cyberbullying is a prevalent issue among female adolescents.

In a report from the Children's Society in the UK, Dr Linda Papadopoulos suggests, 'Boys are more overt on social media, whereas girls bully by exclusion, which means there is an elevated chance for girls to be perpetrators and victims.'[3]

Body and fat shaming, racism and pornography, poor sleep patterns, and increased rates of depression and suicide are the dark realities for females facing cyberbullying, and as a result of women spending more time on social media.[4]

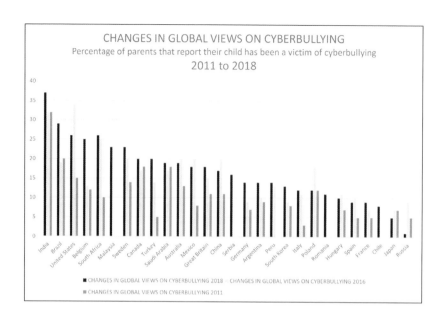

CHANGES IN GLOBAL VIEWS ON CYBERBULLYING
Percentage of parents that report their child has been a victim of cyberbullying
2011 to 2018

■ CHANGES IN GLOBAL VIEWS ON CYBERBULLYING 2018 　CHANGES IN GLOBAL VIEWS ON CYBERBULLYING 2016
■ CHANGES IN GLOBAL VIEWS ON CYBERBULLYING 2011

GENDER PREFERENCES ON SOCIAL MEDIA USAGE

A study from the UK anti-bullying organisation, Ditch the Label, found that 42 percent of surveyed young adults experienced cyberbullying on Instagram. That was compared to 37 percent on Facebook and 31 percent on Snapchat. Perhaps surprisingly, only 9 percent reported having experienced cyberbullying on Twitter.[5]

The detrimental effects faced by girls' and women's self-confidence when social media goes wrong can be catastrophic, and research shows it can lead to self-harm and suicide. When we shine a light on these dark corners of social media, we can find ways to own the solutions and own our confidence again.[6]

Gender-based confidence

Women and men exhibit confidence very differently. Men typically have a propensity to be overconfident, leaving them exposed to failure more often than they should be.[7] Confident women manifest qualities such as emotional intelligence, compassion, being able to actively listen, accept and explore emotions openly and, the ultimate quality of a confident woman, the ability to ask for help.[8]

SOURCE: https://www.dove.com/nz/dove-self-esteem-project.html

Kristen recounts living in two worlds as both male and female growing up before she fully transitioned.

> *Those are social ideas that have planted seeds in our minds of how you identify one sex over the other. We're socially trained that way. So for me in my own personal experiences, through the transition and my experience as Kristen, I've had to realign all those experiences and I've seen it literally from both sides. [...] I have to survive now as Kristen, and I have to live that in a professional world.* **Kristen Worley**

In 2018 the Harvard Business Review researched the confidence gap between women and men. They focused on measuring organisational systems and reported that there was a gap between the self-confidence of women in reality and the self-reported confidence of women. In other words there was a gap between what women reported versus how they actually felt.

Different expectations for women

It can be said that men are held to a lower standard when you compare a male and female doing the same job. This is because underqualified and underprepared men don't think hesitate to *lean in*. Men apply for jobs when they meet only 60 percent of the qualifications, whereas most women would apply only if they met 100 percent of them.

'Successful women cannot *lean in* on a structure that cannot support their weight without their opportunities (and the myth) collapsing around them,' observes Laura Guillen, writer for the Harvard Business Review.[9]

But this is not only about men being overconfident. It's *because* they are confident that the systems are setup to make the other 40 percent come out in their favour.[10]

> *I wanted desperately to be an MP so that my various communities had a voice in decision making. It was never just about me, but people couldn't see that.*
> **Anjum Rahman**

Competence versus confidence was another hot research topic and again the perceived competence of women to men in leadership was overwhelmingly in our favour. Women were rated by men as more effective in 84 percent of competencies (17 of the 19 competencies measured).[11]

Confidence from diverse worldviews

In Chapter Two I raised some of the cultural differences used to describe confidence. For example, what might be perceived as a confident woman in western society may be seen completely differently by other cultures.

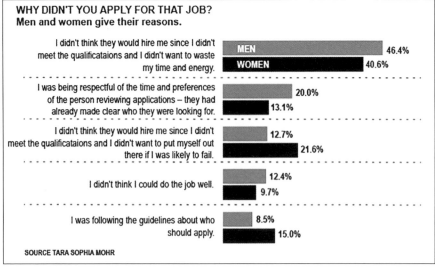

WHY DIDN'T YOU APPLY FOR THAT JOB?
Men and women give their reasons.

I didn't think they would hire me since I didn't meet the qualificataions and I didn't want to waste my time and energy.	MEN / WOMEN	46.4% / 40.6%
I was being respectful of the time and preferences of the person reviewing applications – they had already made clear who they were looking for.		20.0% / 13.1%
I didn't think they would hire me since I didn't meet the qualificataions and I didn't want to put myself out there if I was likely to fail.		12.7% / 21.6%
I didn't think I could do the job well.		12.4% / 9.7%
I was following the guidelines about who should apply.		8.5% / 15.0%

SOURCE TARA SOPHIA MOHR

SOURCE: Harvard Business Review

What about diverse groups *within* a gender category? Are LGBTQ, women of colour, ethnic, Indigenous and disabled women facing the same challenge around confidence? Globally the stats are barely in single figures, so there is a realisation that the current way of attracting, developing and retaining diverse groups of women across the corporate world requires an overhaul.

> *What you may feel is confidence. It may be something entirely different, and you have to be extremely careful. [...] What I've also learned in working with different cultures and different diversities, is what you have to show. You have to be wired in a way to be humble. You have to be wired in a way to be highly sensitive to other people's ways of thinking, coming from different life experiences and be accepting of their thinking and of their values.* **Kristen Worley.**

A growing body of research indicates that those who identify as LGBTQ not only face more significant bullying in person but are also more likely to be bullied online, compared to those who identify as heterosexual. The consequences of this kind of treatment also lead to an increased rate of discrimination and harassment in the workplace resulting in low self-esteem and low confidence.

In 2018, 92 percent of the LGBTQ community surveyed said that society is more accepting of them today than it was in the past. Yet low confidence and self-esteem is highlighted as a major obstacle faced by this group in the workplace.[12]

Addressing confidence and low self-esteem through LGBTQ support services and networks is imperative. Not only can it help this group lead better, more fulfilling lives, but it can also serve as a preventative measure against addiction and relapse.

What can you do to own your confidence today?

Owning your confidence and counteracting these roadblocks, in order to smash through these negative statistics with empowering actions, is what the final part of this chapter is all about. Confidence is taking 100 percent responsibility for and ownership of where you come from, who you are, what you do, the actions you take, how you behave, and everything that comes with that responsibility; the good, the bad and the ugly.

The missing part to all the confidence books Jo and I have read is the 100 percent responsibility and ownership part. And, guess what? When you take 100 percent responsibility for owning your confidence, some people might not like it; they might be people close to you, or strangers who disagree with your perspective. As long as you are ready to own what you put out into the world, I believe the right people will align themselves to you. Start slow, one step at a time; test and then repeat.

Create your confidence cocktail
LET'S START YOU OFF WITH A CONFIDENCE COCKTAIL

THESE ARE THE CORE INGREDIENTS OF CREATING YOUR COCKTAIL
Here's your four-step confidence cocktail recipe:
Step 1. Start by writing down the times in your life you felt at your best.
Was it as a child when you were free and fearless?
Was it when you won your first race at athletics?
Was it when you travelled?
Or when you found out you were going to be a mum for the first time?

Add those special moments to the mix first. These are the base notes of
your cocktail. They form the base of your life experiences giving your life form
and clarity. Remember to only add the goodies that boost your confidence.
Remember, you cannot give what you don't have, so fill yourself with love and
kindness first, then you'll have plenty of what you wish to give.

Step 2. Next you need to add what is important to you. These mixers will flow
through your cocktail and strengthen the flavour, like family, ethics, respect,
aroha (love), Te Reo Māori (Māori language), freedom.

Step 3. Now you need to add something that is unique to you, that will give
your cocktail a twist. For example, I would add Indigenous entrepreneur and
coaching to my cocktail.

Step 4. And finally the cherry on the top. Garnish your cocktail with things
that make you feel confident, like your favourite shoes, outfit or pounamu
(greenstone); something that you wear for special occasions that makes you feel
fantastic. Now shake well!

Throughout this book **Stacey Morrison** has shared some of the ways she demonstrates
her confidence and the words of her mother would definitely be a great addition to her
personalised cocktail.

*I know that sometimes you can exude confidence that's fake. I just settle myself at a
spiritual [level and] know that that is centred and that is real. It's bigger than me, it's
from my ancestors. Who am I to mess with them?* **Stacey Morrison**

Stacey Morrison connects confidence to the words of her mother as a young girl growing up.

*[When I was young I didn't see many people who were like me on television, but]
my mum would always say, 'You're beautiful; you're good at this.' I must admit I
totally would go, 'Oh, that's cos she's my mum. That's just what she thinks.' But I*

THE CONFIDENCE COCKTAIL

STEP FOUR
Add the garnish with your team, your fav outfit, and shake well.

STEP THREE
Add a twist of your uniqueness, what makes you stand out.

STEP TWO
Choose your mixer - your values and your non-negotiables.

STEP ONE
Start with your core base - your best life moments.

Step 1. Start with your core base drink – your best life moments.

Step 2. Then choose your mixer – your values and your non-negotiables.

Step 3. Add a twist of your uniqueness – your uniqueness, what makes you stand out.

Step 4. Add the garnish – your tools, your team, your fav dress or shoes.

Shake well!

Start adding ingredients to your unique confidence cocktail to grow its flavour. Own that drink!

[…] recognise that a lot of people don't have that one voice [saying you're beautiful, you're good] and so if you've never heard those words, how can you say it to yourself?
Stacey Morrison

Ann brings to light a great perspective about divorcing confidence from all the other roles you are succeeding at.

My advice for women is firstly, accept that you're gonna lose your confidence at times and that's okay. It happens to everybody so don't beat yourself up about it. Secondly, when that happens you can take great comfort in remembering your other roles, whether that's because you're a mother or a partner or a friend or somebody's daughter. **Ann Francke**

If you think of confidence on a scale of one to 10, no one is at a 10 every minute of the day. **Ann**'s signature cocktail is about being measured by what you add and don't add. Her counsel is sound.

When your self-confidence is low, at a 2 or 3 out of 10 at work, remind yourself (and others) that you were unstoppable only this morning. This is what my girlfriend shared with me the day I was writing this chapter.

BEFORE	7:30am	Washed and hung out the laundry before
BY	7.41am	Prepared a two-course vegan dinner
BY	7.52am	Picked up the supermarket cake for the first birthday
BY	8.05am	Dropped off all three children at three different daycare centres

The skillset and confidence it takes to do all of that in one hour and five minutes is an example of the uniqueness women bring to this world. Also, having children makes you even more valuable in an organisation. If they don't already recognise and value your Supermum powers then start reading this book again at Chapter One and make a plan to exit that BS. Honestly, when you own this confidence cocktail you will be unrecognisable!

At a recent Islamic Women's Council Conference, **Anjum Rahman** gave the audience 30 seconds to write a list of the top 10 things that they loved in life. It could be people, it could be things, values, whatever they wanted. Around 150 people were in attendance. Then she asked two questions…

> **Question 1.** Where did you put yourself on that list?

> **Question 2.** Who actually put themselves on that list?

Only two or three people had written their names on their list of things they loved in life.

> *So I think my last bit of advice is to put yourself on that list and make sure that loving yourself is a priority. [Recognise] that it's not about thinking that you are better than anyone else. [It is about] just loving you and giving yourself kindness and compassion and self-love. Forgive yourself. Be kind to yourself.*
> **Anjum Rahman**

Anjum's mocktail is a mix of beautiful words that all women need to add from this moment on; they need to put themselves on that list.

ABA – always be aware.

To keep your sliding scale of confidence balanced it is important to do YOU! If 'fake it till you make it' works for you, all power to you. But if that doesn't work for you, know that you're not alone!

Today it really is about growing your own self-awareness; being able to enhance the confidence and authenticity that only you can offer the world. Awareness is 95 percent of the journey to positive change. Do you know what the other 5 percent is? Keep reading. To add to your awareness, I encourage you to first understand your own whakapapa or genealogy. Then expand your awareness to gain new perspectives of other worldviews. When you can stand and talk, with an authentic sense of knowing who you are through your ancestral roots, you own your story, you own your confidence.

The world has become so much more aware of #blacklivesmatter and #racism and the great news about awareness is once you have it, you can't then be unaware. The question then is what do you do with that new awareness? The key is to use that new awareness to take an action.

This is the other 5 percent in the journey of positive change. Taking action.

A lot of women and young girls will go through life collecting mountains of new awareness, but they do nothing with it. Think about it. It might be you, it might be someone you know. I coach women every day who have so much awareness it's mind blowing. Yet they haven't done the one thing they need to do, which is take an action, to complete the 5 percent part of the journey of positive change.

The final part of this formula is that the action needs to be done easily and effortlessly *outside* of your comfort zone.

Using #blacklivesmatter and #racism, here are examples of what you might do easily and effortlessly outside your comfort zone:

- **Have a conversation with a friend who you've never spoken to before about these topics.**
- **Have a conversation with a black, Indigenous, ethnic or diverse person about these topics.**
- **Signup to a webinar or online forum and contribute your point of view for the first time.**
- **Write about these topics and share it publicly.**
- **Interview someone about these topics.**

If you keep doing what you've always done, you'll always get what you've always got.

Be open to alternative worldviews
– a Māori and Pacific lens

By owning your confidence, knowing who you are and where you come from, you can better understand other diverse worldviews.

Through my own worldview, Māori women's participation and contribution in all areas of society is written in the history books, in our songs, in our karakia (prayers) and in our connections as whānau or family to the land, our environment and our iwi or people.

Today we chair and are on the boards of multi-million dollar, Māori owned and operated enterprises, we create quadruple bottom line businesses which measure and report environmental, social, cultural, and economic outcomes to shareholders. According to the Ministry for Women's 2019 report on Māori women in Business, confidence and competence is on the rise![13] Working alongside Pacific Island women in Aotearoa, Samoa and Fiji I'm always humbled by their inner confidence, strength of faith and leadership.

Edith shares her hope for her teenage daughter:

> *My hope is that she takes the world by storm and that the words that we talked about, confidence, knowing your place, knowing why you do it and how you do it, she works that out herself and she doesn't step back from that. She won't be swayed by other voices, other words, other thoughts. She just attacks it and does better. That's the plan. I hope that each generation were just killing it until the next, moving on beyond what I've done. Yeah, that's the plan.* **Edith Amituanai**

A wonderful reading resource for thinking about our next generation comes from Dr Linda Tuhiwai Smith[14] and Dr Leonie Pihama; it is called *Mana Wahine Reader,* volumes one and two. If you want to understand more about a Māori worldview you should read volume one[15] and volume two.[16] As I reread volume one, it gives me confidence that we as Māori women are paving the way for the next generation of young women to step courageously towards growing their own confidence. I hold Linda and Leonie's global research work in the highest regard.[17]

The term 'Mana Wahine' acknowledges a Māori woman in her totality, outside of a colonial paradigm of gender, race, ethnicity and sexual orientation. These two words together connect Māori women to the universe above, the land below, the past and present; propelling us into the future.

The first article in volume one is a poem called 'Don't Mess with the Māori Woman', by Linda Tuhiwai Smith. It talks to the concepts of courage and confidence through the eyes of a Māori woman, and this chorus repeats:

> *Don't mess with the Māori woman*
> *Who stands beside you*
> *As she walks with the power*
> *Of thousands of years*
> *In her blood and her bones.*

The authors **Linda** and **Leonie** bring empowering awareness and a collective perspective to the idea of confidence, supported by researchers, authors, poets and artists. They have provided a resource which shines a much needed light on the impact of cultural confidence in pre and post colonialism from the perspective of Māori men and women.

> *Mana wahine is not, and should never be, considered only about gender relations. It is much more, and moves beyond the colonial definitions of gender identity that is [held within the] notions of biology, femaleness or maleness. Mana wahine is always located within our wider relationships as Māori.* **Leonie Pihama**

As I deepen my matauranga (knowledge of who my ancestors were) and the role of mana wahine pre-colonisation, I grow with a sense of knowing and confidence that I'm on the right path.

Be open to alternative worldviews – a Mapuche[18] and First Nations lens

Mapuche[19] and First Nations women have confidently marched to their own drums throughout history. Under extreme conditions of racism, corruption and abuse, they have continued to activate their communities to embrace change. Māori, Mapuche[20] and First Nations each have unique cultural contexts. Yet the common thread between all Māori, Mapuche and First Nations women is the ability to create opportunity from the most devastating times in history, and respond with hope, vision and action.

The celebration of Indigenous women is how we honour each other and the progress we have made. A great example of how this is done by First Nations is through the work of Roberta Jamieson[21], she is Mohawk and has achieved many firsts: she was the first First Nation woman in Canada to earn a law degree, the first woman ombudsman of Ontario, and the first woman elected Chief of the Six Nations of the Grand River Territory.

Roberta has long promoted greater diversity on corporate boards. She served on the inaugural Gender Equality Advisory Council that advised Prime Minister Trudeau during Canada's G7 Presidency, sat on a number of corporate boards, and is currently on the board of directors of Deloitte Canada.

She has received 27 honorary degrees, earned numerous awards, and is an Officer of the Order of Canada.

There are so many diverse and rich cultures doing amazing work and I acknowledge you all. One day you will all have a place in another book.

Roberta Jamieson　　　Source: ualberta.ca

Practice saying 'no'. It's a full sentence

Are you on automatic 'yes' pilot for everyone else, so when it comes to you there's nothing left in the tank? Do you find the goals or dreams you set for yourself are the last on your to-do list? Or worse, you help everyone else achieve their goals and a year later nothing has changed for you?

According to Oprah Winfrey, 'no' is a full sentence.

- **'No' is empowering.**

- **'No' gives us confidence.**

- **'No' is 'no'.**

- **When you say 'no', you can create space for more 'yeses' that are aligned to what is important to you.**

Bridget talks about getting over her 'no' guilt

> *I said 'no' just yesterday and it's a muscle I've had to train. It's definitely not something that came easily, because normally I'll feel guilt and I'll feel like, 'Oh, how could I say "no" to this particular person, or this family member, or whatever it is?' But I've learned to say 'no'. The reason is [...] there aren't enough hours in the day and if I'm saying 'yes' to you [then] what's falling by the wayside? I really had to exercise that 'no' muscle. The more you use it, the better you get at it. It's like going to the gym. I've learned to say 'no' and every time I do it I feel real stink for about a second and then I feel completely liberated and empowered for the rest of the day. Once you get over that second of guilt you're like, 'Actually, this feels real good. I love this.'* **Bridget Foliaki-Davis**

Saying 'no' takes practice. Make sure not to add 'but' after a 'no'. It completely negates your 'no'. Actually, take 'but' out of your vocab and replace it with one of my favourite words: 'and'. When I first started saying 'no' and getting rid of 'but' it would sound something like this: 'No, and the reason is…' Now I don't bother with the 'and'.

I noticed that people knew where they stood with me. As Brené Brown says, 'it's kind to be clear; it's unkind not to be.'[22]

Arizona talks about building your confidence to say 'no' to work when you're not getting paid what you're worth.

Edith also had to practice exercising that confidence muscle and in regards to work she has some great advice for young women.

I've learned, or I'm continuing to learn, when to say 'no', cos it will save us all [...] heartache, [and] disappointment. I've seen a good analogy – 'You can die from exposure'. If you are constantly exposed to bad experiences, it may save some disappointment later in life to ask 'Is this worth it?' Often I ask that. Is it worth it or worth what I'm doing? Cos it all costs, right? **Edith Amituanai**

Ask yourself, what are the costs when I say 'yes' to this? Costs are not only monetary. You also need to consider the costs to your whānau your time, your health, your emotional wellbeing and your relationships. Everything has a cost. What costs are you willing to pay? How do these costs impact your self-confidence?

If you find yourself saying 'yes' to everything, you are likely to find yourself burnt out, unhappy, tired, feeling used, feeling you're not worthy, or not enough. You will never have time for yourself, you'll feel there is no reciprocity, and you may find yourself asking 'who am I' or 'where am I going'. In the worst cases you will have emotional, mental, physical and spiritual health issues. If this is you, then you are feeling this way because you are out of alignment. Those signs are telling you, you need to own, work, and grow your confidence.

As women, we need to demonstrate to our young girls the positive side of saying 'no'. It relates to consent and how we honour our bodies. Teaching young boys to treat young women with respect, aroha (love) and as equals, is all related to our ability as women to own our 'nos'.

Traci is a great confidence role model and she shares passionately how she does it:

If I was talking to a mentee or [a] person that I was sponsoring, I would tell them that confidence is like a muscle. You keep training and then you can do 3kms and 5kms, and soon you can do a marathon. Growing your confidence over time means you can quieten, mute or turn off those self-doubt questions like, 'Can you really do it, Trace?' **Traci Houpapa**

'No' helps us to create boundaries for ourselves and others. Own your 'no', own your confidence. Practice saying 'no', and then be silent. Don't add any words to validate your decision or justify yourself. Remember, 'no' is a full sentence.

Try on your confidence
GET HYPED

We all need those people around us who affirm us when things are going well, and more importantly when they're not. Many of our awesome women talked about the positive influences they had growing up. Stacey and Brenda spoke about the support they had from family members. We know that this is not always the case, so here is an idea: be a 'hype woman'.

Brenda spoke about the support she had from family members. We know that this is not always the case, so here is an idea: be a 'hype woman' for others. Brenda's son supported her as her 'hype man' and now she now does this for her network of women.

> *[...] This came from my son. [He] said, 'I'm going to be your hype man, Mummy.' I said, 'What's that?' He said, 'A hype man. Don't you know about hype men? I'm here to constantly say things to make you feel good and big you up. This is my job, to be your hype man.' So I now do this for my girlfriends. I don't know what you call it for a woman - a hype woman, a hype chick, hype lady? But I often say to friends, 'Let's be each other's hype chicks.* **Brenda Trenowden**

How cool is that? Decide who you want on your hype team and start recruiting.

Call on each other to hype each other up before you are to present, have an interview, attend a performance review, or a business pitch. Let each other know when you're feeling nervous or maybe lacking that little bit of extra confidence, and start the hype.

> *I've got a friend who has been going through a difficult time recently. She had a difficult situation at her previous job and she's now going for interviews. She is a rockstar. She's such a phenomenal woman, but the situation at her last company has just knocked her confidence[...]. Now, before she has an interview, she calls me and I remind her of all her successes and of all the great things that have been said in the press about her. I remind her how brilliant she is and [...] give her confidence. I hype her up before she goes into the interview or meeting.* **Brenda Trenowden**

GET PHYSICAL

Remember to use your body to help change your energy, depending on what you are preparing for. Power posing in front of the bathroom mirror or just before we go on stage is a technique Jo, Brenda and I all use. If you need to take up more space on the stage this is a great way to get your pose on. It involves physically standing in a superhero or Wonder Woman pose for at least 30 seconds.

I also use a traditional form of karakia (an incantation or ritual of ancient words) to help me. Through karakia I have the ability to call on my ancestors to stand with me, support me and bring forth a spiritual connection to keep me safe. It also gives me a huge sense of confidence to know I am not alone on that stage or in that pitch. It's powerful and empowering.

FIND INSPIRATION

Listening to music or an inspiring speech is a great way to get you to that right level of confidence. Choose a song that makes you feel good and gets into your bones – and turn it up! You often see athletes with their headphones on before a big race or game.

SHIFT YOUR MINDSET

Adopt an athlete persona, if that helps. Don't be too shy to have a boogie in the bathroom. There is a lot of science about changing the state of your mind and confidence through performance, movement and dance.[23]

Before she goes on stage, Beyonce changes into Sasha Fierce to allow her alter ego to take over those parts of her that aren't as natural. Sasha is her fierce, sexy, aggressive, provocative stage persona. 'Run the world (Girls)' is one of my all-time favourite hype songs.[24]

BE AUTHENTIC

Make sure you are pitching your level of confidence at the right point. Over-confidence is not attractive. Authentic, assured confidence is.

PRACTICE

If you have the means to hire a public speaking or media coach I highly recommend it. My first media coach was Maggie Eyre in London. She was brilliant at supporting me in finding the right scale of confidence to tell my story, as I stepped out of corporate and into my own business.

The DIY version is to record and video yourself practicing. This technique has helped me improve 100 fold. It helped me to see myself from a third person's viewpoint and pick up on the ums, ahs and mannerisms that were totally unconscious to me until I saw them on video. Yes it's a bit cringeworthy to start with, but believe me, you will appreciate the value as you enter those stressful occasions, calm, prepared, and… confident.

TELL YOUR STORY.

If you come from an ethnic, Indigenous or culturally diverse background, you will know that storytelling and oratory are part of who you are. Translating your personal narrative, brand and value into your own empowering story that engages others to take action is a critical confidence skill all women should adopt.

The confidence to stand and tell your story, in your unique language, through performance, song or art, is empowering for you and others. World and visionary leaders use storytelling every day to bring people on a journey, to galvanise the troops, to get votes, and to challenge the status quo.

Combining your personal story, with your achievements log, (as Jo shared in Chapter One: Value Your Worth), your unique value, culture and outcomes is a powerful recipe for confidence and success.

Create a new narrative that empowers you to live your best life as a mum, a nurse, a CEO, the Chair, a millionaire, a grandmother, a business owner, a bus driver…whatever you want to be, be the best you can be.

> *Tell yourself a story: 'I am a daughter of this. I am a daughter of a warrior and a descendant daughter of this. The future looks like this for me. My dad worked in a factory for 12 hours, six days a week. This is for him'. Whatever, you need to tell yourself something because there will definitely come days when you're going to hear the bad, the stories that will tell you to not get up, stay in bed, change your career, do something better. You look like this, you should look like that. You just tell yourself something else.*
>
> *Stay close to reality too. I'm not saying go and talk on some delusion, but we need to tell ourselves something and it needs to be drawn from reality, something that keeps you grounded. That might be in the form of an object too. You might need to keep something close to you.* **Edith Amituanaih**

Simon Sinek uses the golden circle to tell powerful stories. It's simple and effective. He draws 3 circles inside each other with the centre being your WHY, the next being HOW and final outer circle being WHAT. The golden circle concept says that everyone can tell you what they do and how they do it, but organisations like Apple tell you WHY they do it which captures the emotive messaging and instantly draws you into their story, their brand. No one really cares how and what you do if you get your WHY right. Leaders have mastered this technique. Simon says, 'People don't buy what you do, they buy why you do it.' It's your 'why' that is the key to this technique. If you know this you are halfway there.[25]

It can be two simple sentences that you use when someone asks you what you do, or to engage an audience, your team, or as a closing statement for your final interview. Checkout the six types of elevator pitches.[26] Once you have found a template that resonates with you, find a platform to share your story. When you share something of yourself through storytelling in an authentic and vulnerable way, you invite others to do the same.

Maya Angelou once shared, 'I've learned that people will forget what you said, people will forget what you did, but people will never forget how you made them feel.' Happy sharing.[27]

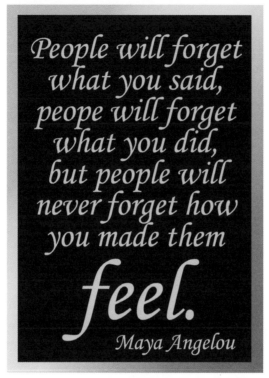

People will forget what you said, peope will forget what you did, but people will never forget how you made them feel.
Maya Angelou

FACE YOUR FEARS AND GET UNCOMFORTABLE

What if fear was your friend? What if understanding your fears and accepting them was the secret to gaining more confidence, and achieving your career, business and life goals?

Feel the Fear and Do It Anyway by Susan Jeffers, is one of my all-time favourite self-help books.[28] If you haven't read it, get it. It is a simple practical read – you could read it in a night if you wanted to. The number one lesson I learnt from this book was that in order to grow and achieve what you want in life you have to step out of your comfort zone. You need to step into uncomfortable or diverse environments to own it, work it and grow your confidence.

The magic you seek lies on the other side of fear. So let's get uncomfortable.

Ninety-five percent of all uncomfortable situations turn out to be learning experiences or positive memories. Yes I made mistakes, I failed at some of the career choices I made, I burnt a few bridges, but overall they were positive life-changing experiences. These experiences supported me to grow my confidence and my hope is they will for you too.

Make a list of where you are stepping out of your comfort zone and feeling uncomfortable. If you can't find anything then you are probably so comfortable that you are in a rut, or not growing personally or professionally.

Being uncomfortable is being the odd one in the room and not worrying about standing out, i.e. the only woman, the only Muslim woman, the only transgender woman, or like **Jackie Clark** you might be at a conference of women and call out the fearfulness in the room.

> *After every speaker [at this conference] there was polite applause. I was up there and I said, 'Do you understand you're at a conference? Your work, most of you, has paid for you to be here. Paid almost $2,000 for you to be here, at a Women in Leadership conference and you're applauding like somebody won a fourth fucking medal, and you don't want to stand out. All I'm seeing here is fearfulness! This is Women in Leadership – why the fuck are you so fearful? And what are you fearful of?'*
>
> *Jo then asked [me], 'What are we fearful of?' My reply was, 'Standing out.' Absolutely standing out. It's the hugest thing. So many women are held back, completely held back, by their own fear, and it's the fear of their own power.* **Jackie Clark**

Anyone who has met the supreme winner of Westpac's Woman of Influence Award in 2018, or 'The Auntie', as she is commonly known, will know Jackie is a powerful, honest and hard-working woman. She works to empower women who have been subjected to domestic violence to take back their power.[29]

Studies show that 85–90 percent of what we worry about never happens.[30] So stop worrying about what everyone else thinks and start standing out and getting uncomfortable.

STOP COMPARING
Some people call it FOMO (fear of missing out). I call it *comparisonitis*. It has evolved into a common pain point for women who typically are users of social media. The concept of comparing your life to someone else's life on Instagram or any social media platform is where the word comparisonitis comes from. With the global boom in social media platforms, we have never been more able to compare ourselves with others.

As at June 2020 there are 3.196 billion people actively using Facebook, Twitter, Instagram, YouTube, WhatsApp, and Facebook Messenger. We spend an average of two hours and 22 minutes socialising online using these apps.[31]

Research has suggested that young people who spend more than two hours a day on social networking sites are more likely to report poor mental health. Young single women are more susceptible to social media addictions as we are generally more social than men.[32]

Constantly comparing ourselves can make us unwell.

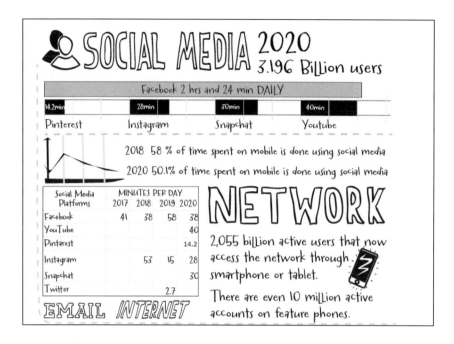

SOCIAL MEDIA 2020
3.196 Billion users

Facebook 2 hrs and 24 min DAILY			
14.2min	28min	30min	40min
Pinterest	Instagram	Snapchat	Youtube

2018 58 % of time spent on mobile is done using social media
2020 50.1% of time spent on mobile is done using social media

Social Media Platforms	MINUTES PER DAY			
	2017	2018	2019	2020
Facebook	41	38	58	38
YouTube				40
Pintarest				14.2
Instagram		53	15	28
Snapchat				30
Twitter			2.7	

NETWORK

2,055 billion active users that now access the network through smartphone or tablet.

There are even 10 million active accounts on feature phones.

EMAIL INTERNET

Taking time out of anything you do on a regular basis is always a good thing: taking time out from work, coffee, friends, family, chocolate, drinking, relationships, and social media etc, helps you to refocus on what is important and what isn't.

Help others be confident
Finally, we need to support other women to 'be' and 'do' confidence in order to get the life they want. In practice the best thing we can do is *be the confidence* for other women and use powerful acknowledgment to help them *be the confidence* for someone else.

When they can't stand using their own power, let's stand alongside them and remind them that they are not alone. When a woman says, 'I'm not good at that,' let's call her out; let's say, 'I'm not buying into your inner critic who's telling you that. It's not true.'

You are courageous.
You are beautiful. You are amazing. You are a leader. You are needed. You are humble. You are strong. You are loved. You are ready. You are right. You are fearless. You are fabulous. You are my hype hero!'

And let's do this for our supportive men as well. John, my husband, has been my time-check wing-man today and it has been so awesome to have his support. I just finished telling him, 'You have been a great wing-man today, thank you.' And let's commit to calling each other out, like Jackie did, when fear of standing out keeps us small and colouring within the lines, just because that's what society has told us to do for centuries.

Now it's your turn to own, work and grow your confidence.

How To Checklist - Own your confidence

- **Create your confidence cocktail.** Have fun with confidence, pour in lots of kindness and compassion and aroha. Reframe confidence and follow the four steps to creating a unique mix that represents who you are; give it a unique twist and share it with the world.

- **ABA – always be aware.** Take 100 percent responsibility for owning your confidence, your voice and your behaviour. The journey of positive change is 95 percent awareness and 5 percent _ _ _ _ _ (the magic word). Whatever you decide, to be _ _ _ _ _ it needs to take you outside of your comfort zone.

- **Be open to alternative worldviews.** Stop and take a look around. If you are not engaging in diverse environments and conversations that look, sound and feel different to yours then now is your time. Start with yourself, do a deep dive and then start exploring other cultures, diversity and conversations.

- **Practice saying 'no'. It's a full sentence.** This is my all-time favourite Oprah-ism. As you start to own your confidence it will get easier, trust me. If it feels hard at the beginning then add 'and this is why…'

- **Try on your confidence.** There are lots of little confidence 'try-ons' that have been tried and tested by our amazing women. Get hyped. Get physical. Find inspiration. Be authentic. Practice. Give yourself a break. You are rewiring years of doing things a certain way, now it's time to try something new.

- **Tell your story.** Every single young girl and woman has a story to tell. Writing this book and adding my story and my voice has empowered me to write another book. Jo and I would love to read your book, watch your movie, read your magazine article one day too.

- **Face your fears and get uncomfortable.** Make fear and failure your friends. To grow and own our confidence we need to let go of our fear of failure. It's okay, everyone fails some time. The magic and the life you dream about lives on the other side of fear. A combination of comfortable and uncomfortable growth is the key to lifelong learning and owning your confidence.

- **Stop comparing.** No one will ever be as awesome, unique and fearless as you are. No matter where you started this journey of confidence, the fact that you are reading this chapter is a huge step forward.

- **Help others be confident.** There is nothing more fulfilling than seeing others own their confidence. If you are the confident extrovert in the room, at the board table, leading an organisation, or volunteering in our most vulnerable communities, make sure you turn around, put out your hand and help another young girl or woman to own their confidence.

Endnotes

1   https://brenebrown.com/books-audio/

2   https://www.businessinsider.com.au/fake-it-til-you-make-it-is-terrible-advice-2014-5?r=US&IR=T

3   https://www.childrenssociety.org.uk/sites/default/files/social-media-cyberbullying-inquiry-full-report_0.pdf

4   https://www.dosomething.org/us/facts/11-facts-about-teens-and-self-esteem#fnref5

5   https://www.comparitech.com/internet-providers/cyberbullying-statistics/#Cyberbullying_around_the_world

6   https://www.forbes.com/sites/alicegwalton/2019/01/05/social-media-again-shown-to-be-worse-for-girls-mental-health-than-boys/#e9678d45057c

7   https://www.theatlantic.com/magazine/archive/2014/05/the-confidence-gap/359815/

8   https://www.huffpost.com/entry/9-qualities-of-confident-women_b_5799710

9   https://hbr.org/2018/03/is-the-confidence-gap-between-men-and-women-a-myth

10 https://hbr.org/2014/08/why-women-dont-apply-for-jobs-unless-theyre-100-qualified

11 https://hbr.org/2019/06/research-women-score-higher-than-men-in-most-leadership-skills

12 https://www.harrishousestl.org/lgbtq-addiction-factors-the-importance-of-self-esteem/

13 https://women.govt.nz/sites/public_files/4218_MFW_Maori%20Women%27s%20Report_final2%20for%20web_0.pdf

14 https://www.zedbooks.net/shop/book/decolonizing-methodologies/

15 https://leoniepihama.files.wordpress.com/2020/01/mana-wahine-volume-1.pdf

16 https://leoniepihama.files.wordpress.com/2020/01/mana-wahine-volume-2.pdf

17 https://leoniepihama.wordpress.com/2020/01/07/mana-wahine-readers/

18 https://www.culturalsurvival.org/publications/cultural-survival-quarterly/bringing-back-balance-women-revitalizing-mapuche-economy

19 https://www.culturalsurvival.org/publications/cultural-survival-quarterly/bringing-back-balance-women-revitalizing-mapuche-economy

20 https://kb.osu.edu/bitstream/handle/1811/86901/KirstenSippola_HonorsThesis.pdf?sequence=3&isAllowed=y

21 https://indspire.ca/about/president-ceo/

22 https://brenebrown.com/blog/2018/10/15/clear-is-kind-unclear-is-unkind/

23 https://www.tonyrobbins.com/mind-meaning/how-to-reset-your-mind-and-mood/

24 https://www.youtube.com/watch?v=VBmMU_iwe6U

25 https://simonsinek.com/commit/the-golden-circle

26 https://strategypeak.com/elevator-pitch-examples/

27 https://www.amazon.com/People-forget-people-Angelou-Decorative/dp/B00KQVSUQE

28 https://www.amazon.com/Feel-Fear-Do-Anyway/dp/0345487427/

29 https://thespinoff.co.nz/society/19-09-2018/congratulations-jackie-clark-supreme-woman-of-influence-and-supreme-aunty/

30 https://www.huffpost.com/entry/85-of-what-we-worry-about_b_8028368

31 https://techjury.net/blog/time-spent-on-social-media/#gref

32 https://www.bbc.com/future/article/20180118-how-much-is-too-much-time-on-social-media

MAKE WORK WORK

– Jo Cribb –

* Work out what you want from work
* Negotiate the hours and conditions you want
* Be clear about what you will achieve at work

As a Chief Executive (CE), I was an advocate for part-time and flexible workers and many of my staff had such arrangements. We managed our workflow by expecting everyone to work on the same one 'pole day' (Wednesdays) so that we could have face-to-face staff and team meetings. Apart from that, we would negotiate arrangements that worked for our employees. We had a skilled, loyal and committed team because they could balance their home and work lives.

But working flexible hours, or less than full time hours, can come at a cost. Part time workers often aren't as valued as their full-time colleagues. Not only will you lose money because you are working less hours, you are likely to lose on the pay scale because you are less valued.

Mixed up in this are a lot of myths and outdated assumptions. The myths of productivity: that if we work long hours we are more productive and that being at your desk equates to being productive (it's got a fancy name: presenteeism); that leaders should always put their job first; and that leaders have wives at home who take care of children and the household. Men at work, women at home, white picket fence.

Many of us – both men and women – do not want our future of work to be ruled by these beliefs and myths.

Work just doesn't work for many of us

Nearly 50 percent of women working in Australia do so on a part time basis (compared with 18 percent of working men). They work on average 17 hours per week (2018)[1]. Similar statistics are found in the UK and NZ.

Nearly 50 percent of New Zealand women working (both part and full time) have access to flexible working arrangements allowing them to start and finish at different times of the day or work from home[2]. Likewise, flexi-time is used by 34 percent of British workers[3].

But working part time comes at a cost. Data from the New Zealand Public Service shows that in 2018, the five percent of public servants who worked part time were paid on average 13 percent less than full-time workers on a full-time equivalent basis[4].

By the time their first child has reached 20, British mothers are earning almost a third less per hour, on average, than similarly educated fathers. Pay progression and promotions are not so open to part-time and temporary workers. As a result, many women on the 'mummy track' missing out interesting and promotion-building projects and the earnings growth associated with staying in a permanent full-time job[5.].

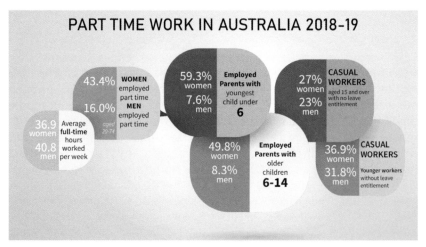

PART TIME WORK IN AUSTRALIA 2018-19

43.4% WOMEN employed part time

16.0% MEN employed part time

36.9 women
40.8 men
Average full-time hours worked per week aged 20-74

59.3% women
7.6% men
Employed Parents with youngest child under 6

49.8% women
8.3% men
Employed Parents with older children 6-14

27% women
23% men
CASUAL WORKERS aged 15 and over with no leave entitlement

36.9% women
31.8% men
CASUAL WORKERS Younger workers without leave entitlement

SOURCE: The Australian Bureau of Statistics

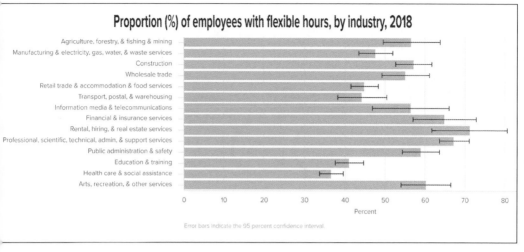

Proportion (%) of employees with flexible hours, by industry, 2018

Error bars indicate the 95 percent confidence interval.

Access to part time and flexible work arrangements are especially important when you are caring for others as well as working. Not surprisingly, parents of dependent children in New Zealand are more likely to have negotiated flexible hours (57 percent) than those without children.

One third of parents (mostly women) reported that they had missed out on promotion opportunities because they used flexible work arrangements[6]. In 2019 46 percent of Australian parents were still saying their commitment to their organisation would be questioned if they even applied for family-friendly arrangements[7].

> *I was selected by the top university in Taiwan and trained to be a diplomat. While female students had the same chance to learn, it was common knowledge that women were never given the opportunities for career progression offshore because they need to focus on the family and marriage commitments.* **Royal Reed**

Thanks to our smart phones, we have never been more accessible to our work and our work has never been more portable. But with this comes the expectations that we are available 24/7. Research showed 76 percent of New Zealand and Australian mothers were looking to change jobs because they could not get the flexibility they needed. The theme throughout the research was that if they did get part time hours, they were still expected to do the work of a full-time worker[8].

Getting flexible or part-time hours might also mean we get precarious employment arrangements. More than 50 percent of women working part-time in Australia were on casual contracts, with no leave entitlement or guaranteed income[9]. Women are more likely to be in low paid and insecure jobs, especially migrant and women with fewer formal qualifications[10].

Some of you will want more hours. The tips in this chapter will work for you as well because the actions we suggest are about changing the terms of your employment to make work, work for you.

PART TIME WORKERS

Individual manager's attitudes and their ability and willingness to manage flexible, part-time teams differ. Even if your organisation has family-friendly policies, it doesn't mean you will be able to access them.

So, it is no wonder so many women are choosing to become their own boss and starting their own businesses. But making work, work when you are self-employed or own your own business is not without challenges. You will be solely responsible for everything, often with little support (unless you can pay for it), you may have to work long and irregular hours to fit around the needs of your customers and clients, all without the safety net of sick pay and annual leave allowances.

So what can you do to make your work work for you?
WORK OUT WHAT WORK MEANS TO YOU
Here's the opportunity you always wanted to play detective. Next time you are out in a social setting where you don't know people, analyse how they introduce themselves to you. I predict that most times people will talk first about what they 'do', meaning what they do for paid work. Hello, I am Sarah, I am a …..

Our paid work is such an important part of our identity. We are office workers, teachers, builders first. We are people later. It is how we make connections with each other and how we size each other up. .

But what do we want from our work? What do you want to be known as? To 'do'? Or to 'be' that is not necessarily defined by how you pay your rent?

Linda tells a story about that. When she was recovering from a serious injury she read a Buddhist poem that said that if you have a glass of water and you put an egg in it, it overflows. If you put the egg in first, then fill it with water it will not overflow. Life is about working out what are the eggs you want in your glass – the things that really matter to you – so that everything else can flow around them.

> *I put having kids on hold to start my first company with the view that I had to sacrifice to succeed. When I got to 'success', I realised that it was completely meaningless. For me, having children, being in a great relationship, contributing to your family, being there for your friends, matter.*
>
> *But here's me: I list my company, I'm worth millions of dollars – but it was meaningless, because I hadn't been to any family events.*
>
> *I thought, you know what, I don't buy this sacrifice and focus thing. I decided that I was going to do everything that I wanted to do at the same time, because what happens if there is no tomorrow? I had two kids. I joined the Red Cross and started my own international social venture and then started two companies, one for my husband and one for me. I never worked more than nine to five Monday to Friday. I never missed another family event.* **Linda Jenkinson**

When I ask my coaching clients what they want from work, many are honest and say they want financial security, especially the ability to pay their mortgage and look after their family. But then when we look at their choices around work, they are not maximizing their earning ability (say by seeking extra responsibilities) or securing their future earnings (by upskilling).

For **Stacey** the most important 'egg' for her was and is her whanau; her extended family. When they are well and relationships are functioning, she is well. If her whanau isn't right, she will get off balance. Knowing this means she works hard to support family members.

For **Brenda** it is about being clear about your priorities: where are you needed most and when. She had to make sacrifices and trade-offs to get promoted but by focusing on what were the most important things to her, she made the best decisions she could about how to spend her time.

You can't have everything all at the same time – of course there are sacrifices. If you want to be successful and you're ambitious and you want to progress, you will have to sacrifice. I remember times in my career when I've missed things at my kids' schools, and I've been really tearful about it. Happily, for me, my husband has been there for most of those important moments. But there are lots of times I've been away and Skyping my daughter on her birthday in the middle of the night from wherever I am or reading my kids bedtime stories from Australia at the wrong time of day for me. But, they've turned out fine - they're really happy and well-balanced kids. They don't remember it and they don't hold it against me.

It's also thinking that when you do have to make those sacrifices, you are clear in your mind at to your priorities at home or in your personal life. If you have kids and you can't be there at everything, you sit down at the beginning of the school year and you talk about, 'What are the key things that you need me to be around for? What are the important dates? And I will move everything I can to be there for those things.' When you're at home you may have to do some work, even at the weekend, but you choose some hours and say, 'I'm going to be fully present and have real quality time with my kids then.'

I'm constantly having to rein myself in on this. So, I sit down and make a list of my own personal priorities: family and friends health, fitness, work priorities, 30 percent work, my boards, etc. I draw these little mind maps, with myself in the middle and all the things around that are priorities. **Brenda Trenowden**

Work out what are the eggs you want in your glass and where paid work fits in this. Ask yourself what does work mean to you? What do you **want** and what do you **need** from your work?

NEGOTIATE BASED ON WHAT YOUR WORK NEEDS FROM YOU

Want to work less? Want to work more hours? Want more flexibility in how you work? Want to work in ways that are different to the way you do now? Okay, so let's talk about how to negotiate the change.

FIRST, START WITH WORKING OUT WHAT YOU WANT.

Then work out why it is in your boss's best interest to give you what you want. Just asking for something that suits you is not the best way to get it. Negotiations always work best if you are working towards a change that suits both parties. Stop and think about what your boss and your organisation needs from you and how this could align with what you want. Be flexible so you can find that 'sweet' spot where what your organisation needs from you matches with what you are looking for.

Giving you flexible hours might mean you start earlier and, depending on the type of work you do, might mean your office could also open earlier so work is done ready for your boss or colleagues when they arrive. Going part-time means you will be able to stay working

in this company, meaning your boss doesn't have to hire and train someone new. Going part-time means your boss may be able to hire someone with different skills to you for the other hours.

Royal's advice, from her employer's perspective, is to focus on the value of your work, not the hours that you work.

> *I see many unsuccessful attempts by professionals, especially professional women, to negotiate based on hours or days, without thinking what their organisation or their supervisor needs. For me it is about balancing what my employee's needs with the demands of clients and court schedules. Too many discussions start, 'I want this arrangement; I want so many days off' without thinking about the employer's needs as well.* **Royal Reed**

SHOW UP WHEN NEEDED

Often there are times of the day or year that are busy or are times when important things happen in a workplace. For example, there may be key meetings – like full team meetings – that are important to be at. There are other times and meetings that are less important.

Analyse your work through this lens. Can you schedule your part-time hours or flexi hours schedule so that you are working at the peak times and so you can be part of the key meetings? This not only makes you more valuable but also makes your absences less noticeable.

WRITE IT DOWN

Do your homework by researching your organisation's policies about part-time and flexible work hours. See if there are other arrangements that are working for other people already. Find out what makes them work well and how they are structured. Talk to other bosses that have approved such arrangements to learn why they are working.

Write a proposal, like a business case, about how your changing the way you work will benefit everyone. Think about the risks from your manager's point of view and how you will help address them. Be clear on what you want and how you can manage your work.

ASK FOR A TRIAL

Suggest to your boss that the arrangements you are suggesting be trialled. Your boss is more likely to say yes if the risk is less; if the arrangements can be changed after an agreed fixed period of time or can be reassessed and renegotiated.

Here is how **Brenda** recommends going about asking for a trial:

> *Explain to your boss exactly what you want to do and be really clear on outcomes you need to achieve. I call it agile working because I think agile has more positive connotations than flexible. Everyone assumes that flexible is part-time but most flexible working arrangements are about shifting work to suit your schedule and still delivering the same output. Some of it may be part-time, but it's not all part-time.*
>
> *Be clear on setting your objectives so it's not about time in the office or input - it's about output. Then say, 'Let's have a trial' and keep checking in to make sure everyone's happy.*
>
> *What you often find after a trial is your boss will realise, 'Actually we're getting as much or more output from this individual.'* **Brenda Trenowden**

When asking for a trial be clear with your boss about what success looks like at the end of the trial and how you will evaluate it together.

SET CLEAR EXPECTATIONS ON WHAT YOU WILL ACHIEVE

The risk of working part-time is that you end up expected to do the same amount of work while being paid for fewer hours. To negotiate a successful change, you need to work with your boss to set clear expectations about your workload. For the trial and after, focus on your performance – what you will deliver. Include clear and measurable outputs so you can quantify your value.

Do not focus on hours. Do not create an agreement that only talks about how many hours you will work. Try to redefine what it means to be a valuable worker in terms of productivity – not hours sitting at a desk. Use your achievement log (as outlined in the **Value Your Work** chapter) to record what you have achieved and what the impact is.

Include in your negotiations and agreement, a development plan. You should have one, the same as your full-time colleagues. Think about the opportunities you need to progress and work them into your negotiation. Include a pathway and expectation for promotion. Remember, the more skilled you become, the more useful you are to your boss. It is in their best interest to keep you learning.

HOLD YOUR HEAD HIGH

Sometimes you may hear the smirk of your co-workers as you come in late having navigated the school drop off. Part time workers and those with flexible arrangements can often be thought of as slackers, who are a burden to the rest of the team. Ignore it. Don't listen or believe any of that BS. Not working Fridays makes you no less valuable than anyone else who does. Your achievement log will prove that.

Do not buy into this crap by apologising for not being at work when you are not supposed to be there.

Do as **Ann** did, walk into meetings late with your head held high:

> *When I was a divorced single mother, I needed to take my daughter to school and my boss agreed. He had a meeting that started at 9 o'clock. Taking my daughter to school meant I would be late for that meeting - I would be there at 9.30. He said, 'That's okay, do that.'*

> *So I walked in late to the meeting. The first few times I was deeply embarrassed and awkward. But then I got used to it and people got used to it, and it was kind of like no big deal.*

> *Because I had known how important flexibility is, when I became a manager, I offered flexibility to my team. They weren't divorced single women, they were talented young people, many of them fresh from university, but one wanted to go clubbing so he came in late and left late. Another wanted to play the violin so he came in early and left early. One day I got a call from head office, 'You know you have the highest shares and margins of any cosmetics and skincare category in the world. I want to come visit you and talk to you because you also have the most gender balanced division.' Flexible working produces results.* **Ann Francke**

DON'T BE HARD ON YOURSELF

Making work, work is hard. Few of us get it right. We are constantly making trade-offs. Sometimes we get the balance wrong and the guilt that comes with balancing caring and work can be like a strangle hold on our happiness. I remember that the deep feeling of guilt only left me when my youngest started school. At least then, I rationalised, the State had decided we should be apart so it is okay for me to work.

Royal shares similar thoughts with us:

> *I'm so passionate about my work and it takes so much of my attention. I have missed the time to support my children. My son is now 17 and doing exams and struggling a bit. I wonder if I had been there more if he would be doing better.*

> *My daughter is now 16 and she's lovely. A few weeks ago, when she was on holiday, I took her with me when I had a whole week in court out of town. On the way there she asked my colleague in the back of the car - 'So what does my mum do at work?'*
> **Royal Reed**

Sometimes work will be the most important egg in our glass, sometimes it will be our family, and sometimes our health or the needs of a loved one. Getting the balance right is hard.

Please don't be hard on yourself. It will all work out in the end. Everything will be okay.

HOW YOU CAN HELP OTHERS

If you are a manager or someone who employs people, you are in a fantastic position to help other women. You can set the tone and culture for those who work for you. Think about the teams you lead now. How many of those that work for you do so part-time or have flexible arrangements? If they don't, why don't they? How could you make work work better for those who work for you?

Balancing Cultural expectations and work

Understanding the breadth and depth culture, ethnicity and diversity bring to the workplace is an ongoing discussion. Policies that recognise different cultural celebrations and protocols promote and improve employee engagement and productivity, yet many employers are reluctant to acknowledge the importance of balancing cultural expectations and work. In New Zealand many organisations including government agencies include tangihanga (funeral) leave for 3 days which is a typical funeral grieving process for Māori. If you are an employer, avoid assumptions about how different diversities and generations prefer to work; and instead speak to your people and find out what working arrangements bring out the best in them.[11]

If you have colleagues that are interested in working flexibly, can you advocate for them? Can you help them make their case? Can you talk to your co-workers on their behalf? Can you be their champion when they are not at work? Can you make sure they get all the information they need to succeed in their roles, information they may miss out on because they aren't there all the time?

You can help everyone by not buying into the myths about productivity and the need to be present for long hours to be productive. Have you ever bragged about how busy you are, how you worked late, how much work you took home? Just don't. It's not a good thing. Countless studies show that length of time working has little correlation to effectiveness and productivity actually declines after 55 hours. When working long hours the quality of our decision-making and ability to communicate drops as well[12].

Brenda has taken to social media to challenge these myths.

> *I am constantly pushing against this whole culture of 'I can survive on four hours sleep.' I am really fed up with leaders boasting about this, so I've started to tweet about the opposite. On Monday I read in the Financial Times about the CEO of an asset management firm who was saying, 'I can do all of this because I can survive on four or five hours sleep a night.' So I tweeted about the fact I didn't want to hear any more boasting about not needing sleep and that 'I had seven hours last night and I would really love a nap this afternoon'. We've got to challenge these people.*
> **Brenda Trenowden**

The part time, flexible work issue is often seen as a women's problem. Trying to juggle raising the next generation of humans as well as make a meaningful contribution to the workplace, while making a critical contribution to our family finances, is not just 'a women's problem'.

Sadly, it will take the 'defeminisation' (yes, I made this word up) of part-time and flexible work arrangements to really see more options opening up and for workers who take them up to be valued. This means far more men taking parental leave, and negotiating part-time hours. So if you are a brave man reading this (and good on you for doing so), please go part-time or arrange your hours so you do the school pick up. And do so proudly and loudly.

Check List for Make Work, Work

- **Work out what work means to you and what you want from your work.**
  Be clear about your priorities and where work fits in (or doesn't) with them.

- **If you want to work less, work out why it is in your bosses interest for you to do so and prepare a proposal based on this.**

- **Ask for a trial.**

- **Negotiate new work arrangements based on what you will**

produce or deliver rather than how long you will spend at your desk.

- **If you work part-time or flexible hours, do so with pride.**

- **Be gentle on yourself.** No one has really cracked this. There is no ideal or right answer, just what suits you.

Endnotes

1   https://cdn.aigroup.com.au/Economic_Indicators/ Research_Notes/2018/Ai_Group_casual_work_ June_2018.pdf

2   https://www.stats.govt.nz/news/over-half-of- employees-in-new-zealand-have-flexible-work-hours

3   https://www.cipd.co.uk/Images/flexible-working_ tcm18-58746.pdf

https://www.robertwalters.co.nz/content/dam/robert- walters/country/new-zealand/files/whitepapers/ generation-gaps-whitepaper.pdf

4   https://ssc.govt.nz/resources/public-service- workforce-datahrc-workplace/#trends

5   https://www.theguardian.com/society/2018/feb/05/ mothers-working-part-time-hit-hard-by-gender-pay- gap-study-shows

6   http://www.aplen.pages.ontraport.net/ WorkingFamiliesReport2019

7   http://www.aplen.pages.ontraport.net/ WorkingFamiliesReport2019

8   https://www.stuff.co.nz/life-style/parenting/111863599/a- fulltime-role-in-parttime-hours-the-truth-about-flexible- work

9   https://cdn.aigroup.com.au/Economic_Indicators/ Research_Notes/2018/Ai_Group_casual_work_June_2018. pdf

10   https://eige.europa.eu/resources/ti_pubpdf_ mh0217250enn_pdfweb_20170503163908.pdf

11   https://www.robertwalters.co.nz/content/dam/robert- walters/country/new-zealand/files/whitepapers/ generation-gaps-whitepaper.pdf

12   https://cs.stanford.edu/people/eroberts/cs201/projects/ crunchmode/econ-hours-productivity.html

STAND UP FOR YOURSELF

– Rachel Petero –

* Get the A-team ready to stand with you
* Know your rights; record and report
* Engage experts to call out the bullies
* Own your shine and your s**t
* Book time out; stepping out is okay

'Go home, you black nigger!' a young white male yelled from his passenger window.

Those five words were aimed at me.

There I was minding my own business, out on my walk in my safe place – or it had been until then. I was 25. I remember being scared that the car might stop up ahead, so I stopped and watched the number plate disappear until I couldn't read the letters anymore.

At that moment, the two words 'black' and 'nigger' brought emotions I hadn't experienced before: shock, anger, shame, embarrassment, inferiority, fear, isolation and total confusion. I remember trying and failing to process them.

Standing there on New North Road, I felt totally violated by those two words. What had I done to make someone shout those derogatory words at a complete stranger? Maybe his mate who was driving dared him to do it? What makes someone hate another person for the colour of their skin?

I didn't tell John when I got home. This is the first time I've told anyone here, in this book.

John and I had bought our first home in West Auckland and our careers were on track. Our jobs in Auckland's CBD were taking off and I had finished my part-time study. John was a budding young engineer, and I was a young Māori woman in a creative design agency with big aspirations and goals. Life was good.

Like many other Māori and Pacific Island families, our parents migrated to Auckland city for work. My parents both came from big families south of Auckland and our tribal lands of Waikato.

Working conditions in the late '60s and '70s were very different from today. I know both our parents faced racism when they moved to Auckland. I'm not sure I would have had the resilience to weather the ignorance and intimidation dished out daily in some of the stories our parents told us. Words like blackie, nigger, coconut, freshie, hori (a derogatory word for Māori), savage and golliwog were loosely thrown around in the workplace. In those days it was seen as a joke, not worthy of a reaction, and certainly not worth calling it out for what it was – a racist remark. Everyone would just laugh it off and carry on with their duties.

My parents made choices and sacrifices for my sister and I, and we now know that they protected us from a lot of the discrimination they faced. They also made sure we knew our cultural heritage by taking us back to the Waikato regularly and often. We were the townies to some of our cousins and whānau. Society called us 'urban Māori'.

I worked out early in life that society wanted to label me. Those labels categorised me as a woman, Māori, black, a statistic, and from that came assumptions such as the expectation that I'm going to be pregnant by 16, a bad mother, a smoker, in prison, in a gang and… and…the list goes on and on.

When I told my mum I wanted to leave school to get a job I'd seen in the newspaper she didn't stop me. She knew I would do it anyway. The job was at The Sun newspaper and – talk about sexist advertising! The job title was 'Girl Friday'. But, I had decided I wanted to be a journalist and my dream at that time was to be a journalist on TV One.

I still remember the grey, black and white shirt dress I wore with my cerise pink lipstick and puffy hair. Full of confidence and determination, I was the only Māori amongst 21 other interviewees. Mike Smith was the manager. He was British and the interviewer. I had no idea what a formal interview would be like. All my part-time jobs had been straight forward – 'Do you want the job?' 'Yes.' 'Great. When can you start?' No CV (Curriculum Vitae) or review of my competence.

I can't remember exactly what I said or what Mike asked. All I remember is that in the office of The Sun in Kingsland that sunny day, my gender, my skin colour, and my culture didn't matter to Mike. He saw me, he listened to me, and he hired me.

It was a pivotal moment in my life and I believe it supported my career trajectory, and my confidence and belief that I could do whatever I put my mind to. From that day forward, I would do everything possible to rip off the labels society wanted to impose on me.

Unfortunately, The Sun newspaper only lasted in New Zealand for 1 year due to lack of advertising. I was made redundant after four months. The silver lining is that I received a $3,000 redundancy pay out which paid for my first car. A bright yellow Ford Escort.

These life experiences set me up to be on the lookout for bullying, racism, harassment, and discrimination, and to stand up for myself.

Women's lives matter

The impact of standing up for yourself, another woman or a cause, can have far-reaching implications that you may never be aware of. To stand and be counted because you feel strongly about human rights issues – bullying, gender equality, sexual violence, body shaming, discrimination or safety in the workplace – is courageous.

There are many ways to stand up and many historic moments where the world has come together to stand for girls and young women (#shematters #womenmarch). At the time of writing this chapter, the world has just stood for #blacklivesmatter, George Floyd and thousands of black lives lost before him.

As the world gathers momentum and marches on social media, in town squares, and across nations, there is also a woman or girl somewhere in the world who is being subjected to bullying, harassment and discrimination (possibly all of the above), every second of the day. And that's only what's being reported. Fear of backlash, shame, judgement and the toll on livelihoods and wellbeing is often the reason for standing down and many incidents are not reported. Acknowledging that everyone's journey is unique, my hope is this chapter provides some clarity as to how you can stand up for yourself and other women.

Sexual harassment and gender discrimination

Since 2017, the global public outcry from #MeToo has had an impact on how industries (from arts to politics and corporations) deal with allegations of sexual harassment, abuse and discrimination made by women. Discrimination may be made on the basis of age, race or colour, ethnicity, sex (including pregnancy or childbirth), sexual orientation, disability, religious or ethical beliefs, marital or family status, employment status, political opinion and being affected by domestic violence.

A recent publication from UN Women defines *sexual harassment* as a form of violence and discrimination rooted in historic power imbalances and a male-dominated culture. It permeates governments, the private sector, international organisations, and even areas of civil society.[1] Leadership and culture change are the foundation for permanent and meaningful organisational and societal change needed to end sexual harassment.

In 2018, the US published an extensive and specific report on sexual harassment of both men and women, including the most frequent location respondents had first experienced sexual harassment. The top three locations for women were in a public space (66 percent of women respondents), at work — including temporary jobs and internships (38 percentage), and at home (35 percentage). For men, in public (19%), at school (14%), and at work, home, and by phone or text (13 percentage).[2]

2018 USA SEXUAL HARASSMENT

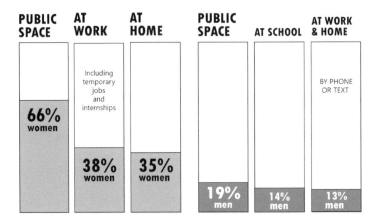

The #MeToo movement has exposed gaping holes in policy, legislation and law reform needed to prevent sexual harassment and abuse in society, including the work environment.

A recent study across 13 countries, by the Ministry for Women in Aotearoa New Zealand, revealed that clear accountability, strong leadership, inclusive policy development and proactive role-modelling from senior staff, needs to sit alongside the promotion of respectful relationships to create an inclusive and empowering organisational culture.[3]

Depending on your country's employment or health and safety legislation, there may be guidelines in the legal framework of your country. If you are suffering from any form of discrimination you must 'armour up' in terms of your legal rights. (There is more on who, what, and how to do that in the last part of this chapter). In the UK for example, harassment is illegal and bullying isn't, under the Equality Act 2010. However, the Health and Safety at Work Act 1974 states all employers have a legal duty to ensure the health, safety and welfare of their employees – which includes protection from bullying at work. Understanding your specific national or regional rights is critical.[4]

There is a high chance, if you're female, that you've encountered some form of discrimination. It can be visible, such as sexual harassment, getting fired because you're pregnant, or being paid less than men. It can also be invisible, like being passed over for a promotion in favour of a someone else, not being hired into a historically male occupation, or not getting offered career-enhancing assignments because you're seen as being on the 'mummy track' (which Jo covers in Chapter Five – Make Work Work). The reality is that over 50 percent of British women have suffered sexual harassment while at work or their place of study, according to a recent report by ComRes.[5]

The *Australian Human Rights Commission 2018* report cited a significant increase of sexual harassment in the workplace. Seventy-one percent of Australian men and women had been sexually harassed at some point in their lifetimes, with more than 85 percent of Australian women (four in five) experiencing harassment.[6]

As the UK and Australia report a rise of sexual harassment, a recent surveyed of 1,400 New Zealand public service organisations found sexual harassment complaints doubled between 2015 and 2017, and was tracking at the same rate in 2018.[7]

The key insights from New Zealand women who found the courage to stand up and speak to were:

- **they blamed themselves**
- **they felt powerlessness**
- **they were re-victimised by the process of complaining**
- **their lives and careers were impacted negatively.**

Universities in New Zealand reported more than a third (36 percent of the total respondents) said they had experienced some form of sexual assault. When the data was broken down by gender, 41 percent of women reported being assaulted and 22 percent of men.[8]

Based on the above sexual harassment and gender discrimination evidence, which we can assume is skimming the surface, we can say that on average women are three times more likely to experience one or both types of discrimination. As we dig deeper into what gets in the way of us standing up for ourselves, we find further layers of abusive behaviour that can be harder to detect, especially in a workplace environment.

Bullying

In the UK, bullying is defined as 'offensive, intimidating, malicious or insulting behaviour; an abuse or misuse of power through means that undermine, humiliate, denigrate or injure the recipient'. According to a recent study in the UK, 25 percent of UK employees are bullied at work.[9]

Bullying starts early in life. UNESCO reports that globally one-third of youth will experience bullying at school. In countries where bullying is highest, girls are more vulnerable.[10] The impact of bullying is well documented and, as we all know, both women and men are affected. The lifetime effects of bullying can lead to behavioural issues, lack of self-esteem, and ongoing psychological and mental health problems.

Bullying, harassment, and discrimination happen to around 300,000 employed people in NZ, or 11 percent of workers, according to a Statistics NZ report in 2018 . Women were more likely than men to have had these experiences, with Asian and Māori ethnic groups impacted most. Across all ethnic groups, women reported higher rates of discrimination, harassment, or bullying than men. The biggest gap was among employed Māori, with the rate of Māori women (17 percent) twice that of Māori men (8 percent).[11]

I have first-hand experience of supporting and coaching a friend through a case of bullying by a senior woman. To put up with this BS from the opposite sex is one thing, but to put up with it from another woman frankly makes me feel sick to my stomach. A group of us stood by our friend for four years as we empowered her to take back her mana (inherited indestructible birth right) and now we see her shining and flying in her rightful space. Her story had a positive outcome. Many don't.

The challenge with bullying (and all forms of discrimination) in the workplace is that it can be so subtle at first that you don't even notice it. Or you might think you're imagining it. Then you start second-guessing yourself; your self-esteem and confidence start to wane, and then your bully pounces. They want to control and overpower you, to take your confidence. And I do understand why you give over your power. It's not your fault.

Managers and leaders have a responsibility to take all bullying accusations seriously and must listen and act on all reported cases. If you feel this is not being done in your situation, escalate your complaint to someone who is willing to listen. By speaking up and standing up for yourself, there is a high chance others will come forward too.

> *I advocate for gender balance on a professional level [because] it's one of the best levers you can pull to make people better managers and leaders. I advocate for it on a personal level because I know exactly how it feels to be the only woman in the room and [to] be the subject of conscious or unconscious bias or bullying.*
> **Ann Francke**

The Advisory, Conciliation and Arbitrary Service (ACAS) in the UK reported that bullying is costing the economy £18 billion a year. Some of the impacts of bullying are increased absenteeism, lower productivity, and poor performance; a third of people who report bullying leave their jobs.[12] There's nothing like a bottom-line figure to get corporations and government to pay attention. More open and transparent conversations about the costs to personal well-being, and in particular mental health, should be the norm.

As if that's not enough to deal with, there has also been a rise in reported acts of microaggression in the workplace, which is another form of discrimination. For 64 percent of women, acts of microaggression are a workplace reality.

Microagression

Whether intentional or unintentional, acts of microaggression signal disrespect and negatively impact women and companies. They also reflect systemic inequality. While anyone can be on the receiving end of disrespectful behaviour, acts of microaggression are more often directed at those with less power, such as women, people of colour, and LGBTQ people.[13]

We know how hard it can be to call out these real and very painful workplace situations. **Brenda** and **Traci** share their realities.

> *I think that if you're in an organisation that allows bullying, harassment and discrimination to continue it can be very difficult to change this culture. I have in the past tried to fight against it and haven't been successful. When I reflect on what hasn't worked for me, it comes down to choosing your battles. Leaving is always an option once you have exhausted everything else. There is no shame in leaving.*
> **Brenda Trenowden**
>
> *Dealing with sexism and harassment in the workplace is not easy. When it happened to me in the early days of my career, I didn't know how to deal with it and I didn't have the support to work through the issues. In one case I just simply left my job because I was so uncomfortable and I didn't know what to do. When it happened again (because sadly that's still how it is), I was able to access the different systems in the organisation to deal with the issues, and was eventually shifted to another job with another team. But that didn't stop it happening in the organisation nor deal with the cultural issues in that business, it simply moved me out of the line of fire, which wasn't great.* **Traci Houpapa**

Brenda and **Traci** are established business women who continue to practice what they preach. We hope it will help you to know that you are not alone – that they were where you are today. Sometimes you just have to leave a toxic environment to realise the costs to your personal and professional wellbeing.

A Glassdoor survey conducted by The Harris Poll identified that more than half (53 percent) of LGBTQ employees reported that they have experienced or witnessed anti-LGBTQ comments by co-workers. Because of this, 47 percent of respondents said that they believed 'coming out' at work could hurt their career in some way, such as causing them to lose a job, get passed over for promotion, or miss out on a key project. I'm sure these organisations didn't employ 50 percent of a person to turn up to work!

So how do we create environments where you can bring your whole self to work?

Intersectionality

When multiple forms of discrimination intersect, combine, or overlap (i.e. racism, sexism, ageism, or sexual preference), unique layers of discrimination are created. Gender equality and equity are multi-layered and a broader, deeper conversation on a case-by-case basis should be considered.

Kimberlé Crenshaw's famous Ted Talk and 1989 paper *Demarginalising the Intersection of Race and Sex* explains this theory.[14] The reality that hit me square between the eyes in writing this chapter was the number of times my own life is *intersected* – sometimes multiple times in a day. As an Indigenous Māori woman I am often a minority within a majority, depending on each situation I find myself in.

KIMBERLÉ WILLIAMS CRENSHAW
SOURCE: WIKIPEDIA

On a daily basis I am asked to navigate conversations around a board table or on a panel about my worldview on gender, race, cultural appropriation, misalignment of values, and how poor leadership behaviour creates layers of intersectionality. Being the lone voice, being misunderstood, being dismissed, being the only brown face, and being female is often the norm. I have learnt to navigate my place to stand up and speak – and that is not always popular. To highlight intersectionality, imagine you identify as an Indigenous or native woman working for a company that announces, 'We're focusing on women in leadership'. You're being implicitly told, 'We care, but only about that part of your identity we are familiar and comfortable with'.

I'd like to share my personal intersectionality worldview. My gender was what the company felt comfortable with, so gender and race were an intersection. I'm also thinking about my cultural protocols, a key part of my identity, and important to my cultural safety, so add culture as another intersection. Let's not forget my worldview of colonisation; it's real for me and for many Indigenous cultures globally. The antidote to colonisation is decolonisation, which allows me to have a say in how I self-determine my way forward in life or in an organisation, and to put my best foot forward within a framework that I understand as culturally safe and inclusive of my worldview, without judgement or prejudice. If each intersection is a circle (gender, race, culture and colonisation), you get interdependent systems colliding to create four areas of intersectional discrimination, where I feel excluded, I don't see myself represented, I have a different worldview and I can't relate.

Despite all good intentions, there's an implication behind the message for women who come from minority, ethnic or Indigenous cultures. 'Wait your turn. We're helping the majority first.' In my personal experience, white women have always been the majority and I have always been the minority.

In New Zealand, I am a big fan of Linda Tuhiwai Smith and her ground-breaking 1999 book, *Decolonizing Methodologies*. Smith traces the history of scientific knowledge as it developed through racist practices and the exploitation of Indigenous peoples, and asserts a challenging vision for how research and education can be used to confront colonialism and oppression.[15] I think it's a must-read.[16] Linda was also my intermediate, middle school, teacher.

In contrast, Dr Ann Milne and her work on 'Decolonising Education') is another woman who has been through her own decolonisation process as a Pākehā (white) New Zealand woman. She is a powerful speaker and now offers her programmes online. Her webinar 'Colouring in your Virtual White Spaces' is a must-watch.[17]

LINDA TUHIWAI SMITH

Intersectionality

INCLUSIVENESS

RACE

CULTURE

GENDER

INDIGENOUS CULTURES GLOBALLY

WORD VIEW / COLONISATION

CULTURAL PROTOCOLS

What's needed is more awareness about inclusion versus exclusionary and exclusive approaches. **Bridget** articulates how intersectionality impacted her life and career as a Māori woman and a chef.

> *It took me until I was in my 20s before I started becoming extremely proud of being Māori – such a patriot of being Māori it's almost not funny. But when you're younger you look for that identity, and there was no one at school that really looked like me. Then I looked towards my career and I wanted to be a chef [but] there were no female chefs in the '80s and '90s. There were older women who were cooking, like Alison Holst or Julia Child, but I didn't look like them – they didn't look like me. I couldn't relate to them, even though I loved them and adored them, especially Julia Child. I love her, but I couldn't identify with how she grew up.* **Bridget Foliaki-Davis**

Through the lens of intersectionality, we can better include deeper and broader conversations for minority or fringe groups in the workplace when we think about gender-focused initiatives.[18] I highly recommended Kimberlé Crenshaw's Ted Talk.[19]

Racism

Racism is defined by the Oxford Dictionary as: prejudice, discrimination, or antagonism directed against a person or people on the basis of their membership of a particular racial or ethnic group, typically one that is a minority or marginalised.[20]

I wanted to end this chapter with racism for two reasons. I started my story with reference to racism, but it deserves its own space in this chapter. Racism is unacceptable in any form and we are all racist to a degree. Racism to me is like a poison that has seeped into generations of historic DNA, that favours the privileged masses and deprives the marginalised minorities.

The antidote for this poison has three fundamental ingredients:

1. **Youth or age. Bring new generational thinking and innovation to an old conversation.**
2. **Tika, Pono, Aroha. Be the Truth, Honesty and Love in your stand against racism.**
3. **Stand and use your voice for good. Take action on social media, march in the streets, sing for inspiration, build tribes of like-minded supporters.**

The racism conversation is not new for Māori and many Indigenous cultures. It is a conversation that regularly rears its ugly head in media, schools, government, boards and industry.

CLOCKWISE: Rosa Parks;
Mamie Till Mobley;
Rev. Dr Pauli Murray;
Diane Nash;
Maude Ballou;
Coretta Scott King;
Claudette Colvin

STRONG BLACK WOMEN

Women have stood up against racism throughout history, strong black women like Rosa Parks[21], and unsung heroes throughout the Civil Rights Movement, like Rev. Dr Pauli Murray, Mamie Till Mobley, Claudette Colvin, Maude Ballou, Diane Nash and Coretta Scott King.[22]

Women stood in New Zealand too, following the 1893 right for women to vote, led by Mangakāhia of Te Rarawa[23], committees of Māori women were formed in the 1900s such as Ngā Komiti Wāhine. The 1950s saw the formation of the Māori Women's Welfare League, which continues to stand for the rights of women and to hold the New Zealand government accountable to honour Māori and Te Tiriti o Waitangi (The Treaty of Waitangi).

TOP LEFT: DONNA AWATERE   TOP RIGHT: MONA PAPALI'I
ABOVE: MERATA MITA   RIGHT: DAME MIRA SZASZY

Māori protest movements emerged in the 1960s and continued against a background of international and national surges in protest activity. Anti-war, Indigenous rights, black consciousness and women's rights movements all emerged during this period.[24]

Donna Awatere, Mona Papali'I[25], Merata Mita[26] Mira Szaszy (later Dame Mira) are all names synonymous for standing for Māori and women's rights, and fighting colonial attitudes and institutional racism within the New Zealand government.[27]

As Māori and Indigenous women, we continue to take our space and stand up for our Indigenous rights. We are changing the conversation globally for the next generation of young women, ready to stand together and fight the poison of racism.

Actions you can take to stand up for yourself

First, take a breath. Know that you are not alone in this fight against racism, bullying, harassment, and discrimination. The more you share, talk, and stand up for yourself, the more you empower other women and girls to do the same. This chapter, in particular, is also for young boys and men to read and, more importantly, consider how they can take action to stand up for women and against bullying, harassment, discrimination, and racism.

Depending on where you are in your specific circumstances, you can pick and choose what works for you, but always check your National Employment Law Act and your relevant country's legislation on bullying, harassment and discrimination.

Dial a friend, support crew, or your tribe

No matter what anyone says it's never easy to be part of a bullying, harassment and discrimination process. You absolutely do not want to go through this alone. You need a support crew of rational, trusted, judgement-free friends and family – even if only for a good old-fashioned venting session!

STACEY MACKEN
SOURCE: DAILY MAIL

Your support crew can be one great friend or four or five awesome humans who have your back. Typically these situations are long and drawn out. Having a range of people to call on can lighten the load for all. Do not underestimate the mental and emotional resilience you need to get through this chapter in your life. Go into it with your eyes wide open and be as aware as possible of what you are stepping into.

Referring again to my friend who I supported through a bullying case – Stacey Macken not only won her £4 million discrimination suit against her employer (a French bank based in the UK who wouldn't pay her the same as her male colleagues), her courage created a movement that other women believed in and supported too. It took over 12 months for the investigation to take place, mediation to be actioned, and then negotiation between employer and employee to be settled out of court. She did win her case but at a cost to her personal and financial wellbeing. Throughout that time and the following three years, she had different check-in points with her support crew depending on her need. My friend had a long-term goal and aspiration that kept her focused, motivated and moving forward.

Resilience, fierce determination, and your mana (inherited indestructible birthright as a woman) or superpowers will get you through. You must protect your mana and hold onto it. When you are in control of your future destination, whatever the outcome, you will be the winner. When you can, look forward and ask yourself what you want your future to be like. How will it be different? What will be different about you? What are your non-negotiables?

My friend Stacey won her discrimination suit, but she experienced trauma and mental anguish.[28]

> [...] a number of senior women, and this was led by Moya Greene who was the former CEO of the Royal Mail, took out an ad in the Financial Times saying, 'Metoopay, we support you Stacey'. So it's about more women advocating for other women who are mistreated and harassed, and paid less than their male colleagues. And shouldn't be. Ann Francke

Standing up for yourself takes courage and weighing up the benefits versus the costs to you and your wellbeing is an important conversation to have with your family and trusted support crew. Ask yourself, where do I want to spend my energy? Why is this important to me? How will this impact me, my family and my career? The answers to these questions will support you as you prepare to stand up for yourself. Another way to prepare is to educate yourself about your legal position, and to understand your mental and emotional wellbeing.

Know your rights

Do your homework. Get crystal clear on your employee rights before you speak to Human Resources. I always recommend that women have a copy of the policies for bullying, harassment and discrimination on hand, along with your employment contract and job description. If the s**t hits the fan the last thing you will want to be doing is searching the intranet for policies. Once you are clear in your mind regarding the company's policies, processes and health and safety rules you are in a stronger position to stand up for yourself.

Steph Dyhrberg, one of New Zealand's top employment lawyers,[29] is passionate about supporting women who have suffered bullying, harassment and discrimination, and believes allegations of harassment or assault should trigger a 'health and safety response' for women: 'I have a plan, I have a process, I have risk management tools.' I think this is great advice for women and it is a proactive way to prepare and know you have tools at your fingertips to take action or support someone else.

Based on your situation, make sure you have a broad plan for what you would do in XYZ scenario, then, what process needs to be followed based on the company's policies and procedures. Also decide what tools do you will need to mitigate and manage your risk as an employee. An example might be to ensure you have an external free phone number to call for employee relations advice.

Human Resources may or may not get involved from the outset. Whatever happens in those early stages, make sure you invite a work colleague or one of your support crew to your meetings to document or record the conversation.

Bullying, harassment, and discrimination are a Health and Safety risk for all organisations. There are costs to productivity, performance and culture involved, and the bottom line is at stake when bullying, harassment, and discrimination are overlooked or under resourced. Rather than spending resources and time on being the ambulance at the bottom of the cliff, wouldn't you rather see investment in treating the symptoms of this illness? As leaders and managers, you have a responsibility to report health and safety risks at all levels.

Get independent expert advice

Once you have your posse and a plan in place, you should seek expert advice from trusted third parties.

1. *Get recommendations for the right type of legal advice and invest in the best you can afford. Make sure you check any contractual obligations before signing anything – legal advice can be a significant investment, but your reputation and livelihood are worth every cent. Check payment terms and conditions.*

2. *Seek professional emotional support early – a counsellor, a coach or mentor. If you don't have the finances, then Google is going to be your best friend. Scour the internet for free and reputable advice. In New Zealand we have free government services for employees, like Citizens Advice Bureau and the Ministry of Business, Innovation and Employment, who advise employees at no cost.*

3. *Build your A-team of experts – friends, family, tribe, legal, sisterhood, coach, mentor, or therapist, to name a few key team players. Their role is to support and strengthen your case by staying physically, emotionally, mentally, and technically sound throughout. You may also have a financial advisor or an elder on your A-team.*

4. *Once you have your A-team recruited, hold a meeting to update everyone on your situation. Add them all to your speed dial and email. At different stages, you will need to connect to different team members. Check that they are comfortable with this arrangement, or agree how they prefer to be communicated with and with what frequency.*

Call out bad behaviour

If you are noticing behaviours in your organisation that could lead to women being bullied, harassed or discriminated against, you have a duty of care to call them out. I know this may feel like a stretch for some of you, but nothing changes if you don't stand up for yourself and other women. Calling out bad behaviour can mean addressing the specific incident personally or by reporting it to the CEO, Human Resources team, your manager or team leader.

You don't have to be confrontational if that is not your style. You do need to give factual, accurate and objective details about the incident you witnessed.

Mediation is a common practice in organisations, used for opening up the dialogue of what behaviour is acceptable and what is not. Another way of addressing behavioural issues is to request employee training that specifically looks at unconscious bias, cultural competency, and the impacts of discrimination.

Anjum shares her views on breaking down systemic behaviours in politics.

> *I was invited to speak about racism and discrimination within the local body election process. The system is set up to reward certain types of behaviour [and] that needs to be dismantled. I personally don't understand why politics has to be so combative and aggressive. Women can do politics in our own way – in a consensus model. What's so wrong with that?* **Anjum Rahman**

Bridget focuses on turning bullying into a strength she can draw on, to stand up for herself in a male-dominated industry. She literally 'takes no crap.'

> *I've had some bullies in the kitchen, oh gosh, I think back now, 'Oh, please'. Because literally I'm like, 'You had no idea what it was like to be this little Pākehā-looking teenage girl getting bullied by these big girls at school. You're trying to bully me now? Forget about it.' [laughs] Please give me a break. It set me up to take no crap and my 'take no crap radar' is always on. I can sense [crap] a mile away.* **Bridget Foliaki-Davis**

Own your shine, own your s**t

When one woman takes 100 percent responsibility and stands up for what she believes in, she automatically gives other women permission to do the same. You never know who is watching, who is inspired, and who needs you to stand up when they can't. Taking 100 percent responsibility is doing what is right regardless of the outcome. It means standing out, going against the grain, not always being liked, and potentially being judged.

Jackie stands for woman in abusive and violent relationships every day.

> *I say it all the time actually: own your shine, own your shit. You have to own your shine. It's okay to own your shine. In fact, it's imperative to own your shine. Because when you own it, other women, other gender minorities, other people who might not have as much power as you do, who think they don't have any – those people watch very carefully. When you own your shine, they feel like they're able to shine as well. Yeah, that's what that is to me. Women have often said to me, 'I'm really proud of you, blah, blah, blah,' but actually what's more impactful to me is when they say, 'I can do this now, because I saw you doing it.* **Jackie Clark**

Standing up for other women and permitting women to do the same is what Jackie does every day in her community. She also role models how to own her shine by taking 100 percent responsibility for her words and her actions, and empowering other women to do the same.

Diverse role models are important for women and girls to see. If you can't see it, it doesn't exist. Owning your shine is all about not being afraid to let down your armour and shine from the inside out, in all your vulnerability, acknowledging the good, the bad and the ugly. It means others might see your s**t and know you're not perfect. Newsflash – no one is.

Document everything

The reality is that the bullying, harassment, and discrimination may have already happened without you initially picking up on it. Often these difficult situations can arrive without warning and feel like a slap in the face. Providing accurate and objective documented detailed evidence is critical. Think of yourself as a forensic investigator who writes factual step-by-step stories. Leave no rock unturned.

This documentation part is critical and can be time-consuming, but it needs to be done if you want to prove bullying, harassment, and discrimination are real. You need to find a way to document everything you are seeing, hearing and feeling by date, time, location, and include witnesses or who else was there at the time of each incident.

The situation is not going to get better without you being proactive, keeping date-stamped records, journals, diaries, and taking a stand for your personal and professional wellbeing.

There are now apps that you can use to record sessions if you want to use technology to keep records, or you can use the voice recorder on your smart phone to make notes. Save documents in a personal folder on Google docs or Dropbox, and keep your records up-to-date.

Book regular time off

Promise me you will do this. You need to plan time out of the business to take care of yourself throughout this process. (I cover this idea in more detail in Chapter Eight: Put You Mask On First).

Do what you need to do to de-stress. During times of stress, your body builds up cortisol, the stress hormone. Find ways to release those stress hormones. By physically moving your body you release endorphins, your natural antidote to stress. Walking, bike ride, do yoga, stretches, breathing, practise mindfulness, running, sport, dancing, performance – there are so many free ways to release those stress hormones and bring in the happy ones. A routine of 30 minutes a day is all you need but do more if you can!

Work from home or other neutral spaces when you can. It may be mandatory to work from home throughout an investigation.

Make sure you are not exposed to the person you allege is causing you stress. Push for Human Resources or a senior supportive manager to set up a safe working space for you. Don't take 'no' for an answer. If you feel you are not being supported internally then expert independent advice would be a next level step. It's your safety at risk here, so be diligent.

With your team in place, create off-site time to look at your situation from a different perspective. Have you heard the saying: take a helicopter view? It means to step out and look at your situation from above, in the 'third person', or sometimes it's called a bird's eye view. From this perspective, you can discuss and walk through the situation with your trusted A-team or support crew and discuss different scenarios which will provide more clarity around what is the truth and what is circumstantial evidence. Seeing yourself and role-playing each incident can help you to see the entire situation from someone else's point of view, versus only one perspective.

Stepping out is okay too

There is no shame in stepping out – in leaving. Sometimes it's the best thing you can do for your career and your overall wellbeing. If you are one lone voice without support from the top, that is an indicator of how tough it might get. Continually reassess your options. Is it worth it? How far and how long are you willing to fight? Do you have the right people around you to go the distance?

Humans don't naturally gravitate to change. It can feel like you are one person pushing a giant boulder up a steep rocky mountain. Having a few champions and advocates to take a few small rocks up the mountain first can be more sustainable. Many small rocks can create the illusion of one big boulder.

> *In the UK, the Lloyds of London insurance market has had lots of press about the difficult culture there. This week the CEO came out talking about the results of a survey and examples of sexual harassment [and] drinking culture that they are cracking down on. The former CEO, Inga Beale, tried to change things. It was too big a challenge. She was one person, even though she was the CEO, trying to shift the whole culture.*

> *So, I guess it's knowing when you have enough support and when the organisation is open to hearing about your situation and cracking down on it. And when they're not, you have to leave.* **Brenda Trenowden**

Ann stood up for herself as she pioneered and powered through her corporate career, only to discover that it was time to not only move out but also move home and support the family who needed her leadership qualities in a new way for a while.

> *After three of these roles in succession, of being the first and only woman in C-suite, I took a break. I [had] just moved with my husband and daughter to the US. I helped my mother look after my father and I showed my daughter America. She was 15 and she was out of British school just before she would've started her GCSEs, in a huge 3,000 strong state high school in North Carolina. [So] I took a break from the corporate world.* **Ann Francke**

How women can stand up for each other

With world leaders like Malala Yousafzai, Michelle Obama, Ellen DeGeneres, Oprah Winfrey, and New Zealand's Prime Minister Jacinda Ardern standing and speaking out about the inequalities women and girls face every day, the time to uplift each other is now. If we don't, who will?

PANIA NEWTON

I admire young women like Pania Newton a young Māori Activist, lawyer and now mother, based in South Auckland, New Zealand, who continues to fight and stand up for the future of her children, her grandchildren and the return of her land at Ihumatao.[30]

Many women have stood for me to ensure I could stand for myself. They include my mother and my grandmothers – their lessons and legacies live on in me. The permission we often seek externally, to live a full and purposeful life, exists within our identity, our beliefs, our culture and our life experiences.

Now it's your turn to do your part – whatever that is. If the legacy you want to leave is to be the best mum you can be, then do that. If it is to be the CEO of a corporate multinational organisation, then do that. If it is to transform and lead communities and families to better futures, better employment, better environments and ultimately happier, healthier, safer lives, then do that. Whatever it is for you, please do it. Every one of us has a responsibility to stand and support ourselves and other women.

I encourage you to stand for someone who can't stand for themselves. Isn't that what it's all about? That we never feel alone in this marathon that is life. There is hope on the horizon in the workplace, with great examples of collectives coming together to say no more. The power of the people's voice is driving transformation and new opportunities for women and girls around the world. Get involved in some small way, it can make a big difference to many.

> *[…] when it came to light that [Google] had paid $90 million to somebody who was a serial sexual harasser, and 20,000 Googlers walked out and shared their stories of harassment, […] the CEO is like, 'Wow, I have to deal with this. Okay, I have to change the policy.' So collective advocacy by employees for their colleagues in their own companies, and for women in other companies, is going to be on the rise and we*

are going to have more and more mechanisms and routes to help each other. I think that's absolutely necessary. Again, look at the Presidents Club. The expose last year in the Financial Times of hostesses that were hired and made to sign [non]disclosure agreements so they could be groped and harassed. The undercover reporter shed light on that, and that was shut down. Or Ted Baker, where the behaviour of the [CEO's …] serial harassment was exposed. I think more and more of these things are going to be coming to light publicly, and the people are going to speak up. And that's great. **Ann Francke**

How To Checklist - Stand up for yourself

- **Call in your favours.** Build the A-team before you need it. Your team can include your best friend, family, tribe, legal and financial advisors, coach, mentor, therapist, elder or community leader.

- **Run the marathon not the race.** It can be a long and drawn-out process and, when you are working through racism, discrimination, bullying and sexual harassment, you want you to finish strong, so take regular stops along the way.

- **Know your rights.** Get the internal policies and processes clear in your head first, have an independent person with you for any meetings that require a third-party perspective, engage Human Resources as and when required

- **Support, record and report.** Support the person being abused or attacked. Record the incident safely. Report the incident to authorities as soon as possible.

- **Get independent professional expert advice.** Hire the best professionals you can afford: legal and financial advisors, mental health counsellor, life coach, behavioural psychiatrist.

- **Call out and report bad behaviour.** Shine a light on bad behaviour through HR, senior management or a team leader. Make sure you are accurate and specific when you document the incident.

- **Own your shine and your s**t.** Women and girls need to see you role model what you do, how you do it and what it looks like, so they can do it too. Take 100 percent responsibility for the s**t you do too. We all have s**t. No one is perfect.

- **Be a forensic investigator.** Tell your story. Record, document, date stamp, and write accurate, objective, details of each incident involving bullying, harassment, and discrimination.

- **Book time off.** Take care of your emotional, mental, physical and spiritual wellbeing. If you need to, work in neutral spaces or from home to ensure you are not exposed to more bullying, harassment, and discrimination.

- **Stepping out is okay too.** Weigh your options. Ask yourself, have they got your back to do the job you came in to do, or are you being fed lip service? What is more important and what are the costs to you, your health, your whānau your life?

- **Help others up.** Women and girls need to shine and raise the bar by standing up for others when they can't stand up for themselves. Work for the collective and do your part to eradicate bullying, harassment, and discrimination.

Endnotes

1   https://www.unwomen.org/en/digital-library/
    publications/2018/11/towards-an-end-to-sexual-
    harassment

2   http://www.stopstreetharassment.org/wp-content/
    uploads/2018/01/Executive-Summary-2018-National-
    Study-on-Sexual-Harassment-and-Assault.pdf

3   https://women.govt.nz/sites/public_files/Lit%20
    scan%20on%20workplace%20sexual%20harassment.
    pdf

4   https://www.personneltoday.com/hr/is-it-time-for-
    specific-anti-bullying-legislation/

5   http://news.trust.org/item/20171025140717-09jrn/

6   https://www.theguardian.com/world/2020/mar/05/
    employers-should-be-responsible-for-ending-sexual-
    harassment-at-work-australian-inquiry-says

7   https://interactives.stuff.co.nz/2019/02/metoonz/one-
    year-on/

8   https://www.stuff.co.nz/national/113090659/a-third-
    of-women-university-students-report-being-sexually-
    assaulted-what-do-we-owe-them

9   https://smeloans.co.uk/bullying-in-the-workplace-
    statistics-uk/

10 http://uis.unesco.org/en/news/new-sdg-4-data-
    bullying

11 https://www.stats.govt.nz/news/one-in-10-workers-
    feels-discriminated-against-harassed-or-bullied-at-
    work

12 https://www.agencycentral.co.uk/articles/2016-05/
    uk-workplace-bullying-problem.htm

13 https://leanin.org/women-in-the-workplace-
    report-2018/everyday-discrimination-
    microaggressions

14 https://chicagounbound.uchicago.edu/cgi/
    viewcontent.cgi?article=1052&context=uclf

15 https://globalsocialtheory.org/thinkers/linda-tuhiwai-
    smith/

16 https://www.zedbooks.net/shop/book/decolonizing-
    methodologies/

17 https://www.annmilne.co.nz/ann-milne-paid-webinar

18 https://www.ywboston.org/2017/03/what-is-
    intersectionality-and-what-does-it-have-to-do-with-
    me/

19 https://www.ted.com/talks/kimberle_crenshaw_the_
    urgency_of_intersectionality

20 https://www.lexico.com/en/definition/racist

21 https://www.biography.com/activist/rosa-parks

22 https://www.history.com/news/six-unsung-heroines-
    of-the-civil-rights-movement

23 https://nzhistory.govt.nz/women-together/theme/
    maori

24 https://teara.govt.nz/en/nga-ropu-tautohetohe-
    maori-protest-movements/page-1

25 https://teara.govt.nz/en/photograph/27912/
    challenging-racism

26 https://e-tangata.co.nz/reflections/merata-a-sons-
    tribute/

27 https://nzhistory.govt.nz/women-together/theme/
    maori

28 https://www.theguardian.com/business/2019/sep/11/
    female-banker-wins-gender-bias-case-after-witchs-
    hat-left-on-desk

29 https://www.newshub.co.nz/home/sport/2019/05/
    super-rugby-2019-qc-steph-dyhrberg-urges-south-
    african-victims-to-come-forward.html

30 https://www.teaomaori.news/birthing-new-age-
    ihumatao

GIVE AND TAKE

– Jo Cribb –

* Negotiate shared housework and childcare
* Drop your standards
* Ask for help
* Don't try and fix everyone

It was just before Christmas, I was beyond tired – you know that woozy feeling you get from just doing too much – and I was sitting in front of a pile of presents for my partner's family ready to wrap them, when it struck me. Why did I need to think about what they needed, buy them, wrap them and even send them?

I don't think anyone needs a PhD in womanhood to be able to wrap presents. But there is an unwritten and unspoken expectation that women will do hours of this invisible work. Emotional labour it is sometimes called: the work that needs to happen to ensure everyone is happy and comfortable. It is unseen work that glues families and communities together. Christmas usually means we are doing over-time.

Why did it take nearly two decades of doing everything for his family for every birthday or Christmas to stop and ask why aren't we sharing this?

I think we take it upon ourselves to be solely responsible for making happy memories for our family and seek to achieve this through present-buying and serving the fanciest of food. We somehow believe that only one family can have a magical Christmas, so we need to beat every other woman's efforts to make sure that it is ours. We pit ourselves against each other to prove that we are the best mothers / daughters / partners.

We fight our exhaustion to do 'just one more thing' to prove our worth: just one more present under the tree, just one more dessert, just one more drinks party for friends, and so on. The result is we spend too much, buy stuff we and the planet don't need, and are too tired to enjoy our family or ourselves.

How come sending a birthday card needs a PhD in womanhood?

The numbers don't lie. Women do the bulk of unpaid work in our households, regardless if they work full-time or not. The last time Statistics New Zealand counted unpaid work (2006), they found men who work the least paid hours are the least likely to help around the house[1]. Same sex couples are not immune, either. A study in 2016 showed that female tasks and expectations are assigned to the partner who has the more stereotypical feminine traits[2].

As a positive, men are spending more time with their children, but this doesn't include keeping house. Women still do more than 60 percent more unpaid work that men. Swedish research shows even when dads stay at home full time, their working partners still do more than 45 minutes housework a day, on average, than they do[3]. In another Swedish research project, it was found that women who do more housework report that they are less satisfied with their relationships and there is a strong link to divorce[4].

We have all seen the 'dads babysitting their kids' headlines being called into question. Portraying dads as babysitting their children – a short, timebound, voluntary activity – ignores that they are equally responsible for the care of their children. Men can also be portrayed as 'helping out around the house', like a fairy godmother, rather than equally sharing in the responsibility of running their household.

Ever get the sense that you should feel thankful that your bloke did the vacuuming? At test for you: have you ever said thanks to a man for doing a basic chore? Do you get the same thanks in return every time you do something around the house?

Another test: if your partner did a chore, did they do it because they saw it needed doing or because you asked them too? Are you doing all the '*worry work*' – the thinking and planning – as well as most of the actual housework? Studies show that we do much more of the

intellectual and mental work of household maintenance, like deciding what we eat each night or who will collect the mail when we are on holiday)[5].

When it comes to children, again women do the bulk of the emotional labour and child-care. Even before women give birth, we have already started taking up the load – preparing and planning for the new arrival, working out things like sterilizers, nappies, or doing all the reading on child development.

One percent of UK dads took up the parental leave they were eligible for[6] and only five percent (or one in twenty) Australian dads[7] did. Many want to be more hands on fathers in the early days of their children's lives but are either not supported by their employers or can't financially afford to do so. Media and social commentary can also be harsh about dads looking after their kids. It seems no-one is winning from the current way we do things: dads, mums or our kids.

Women continue to do the bulk of childcare as their children get older. Mothers with children under five years old spend around 41 hours a week on childcare and 32 hours on household work, while fathers spent about 17 hours on childcare and 15 hours on household tasks. Once children are older, mothers step up their involvement in paid work but still keep the main responsibilities for looking after their kids[8].

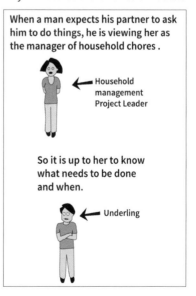

When a man expects his partner to ask him to do things, he is viewing her as the manager of household chores .

← Household management Project Leader

So it is up to her to know what needs to be done and when.

← Underling

At work, our emotional labour continues, for example think about the last time a colleague was farewelled. Who bought the 'Good Luck for your next job' card and smuggled it around to get it signed?

The term 'emotional labour' was first used to describe the work that flight attendants do; not only do they bring us coffee, but they make sure we are calm and have a pleasant flight. Being nice to people all day is hard work. Women are over-represented in many of the jobs that involve large amounts of emotional labour: customer service, caring for the elderly, nursing, teaching and even sex work. When men work in these roles they are often in positions of authority, so it is still women doing all the comforting and caring[9]. So even at work, we are caring for others.

There will always be dishes to be washed and beds to be changed. We never stop caring and worrying about our kids, regardless of how old they (or we are). There will always be someone who needs to be helped out at work or a morning tea to organise. It is often relentless, repetitive (how many times have you washed those same towels?), often unnoticed and expected.

Here's what can we do it about
FIND THE RIGHT PARTNER AND THE RIGHT COMMUNITY
While our women came from different backgrounds, countries, even generations, all agreed on the importance of finding the right partner.

For **Ann**, the right partner is one who respected her wish for financial independence and career aspirations. The right partner for her had to be someone who would share childcare and house work responsibilities.

> *Picking the right partner is incredibly important. Having a partner that is going to respect your career and respect your financial independence is very important. My financial independence was difficult for my first husband to accept. He was a German banker and he said, 'German bankers do not relieve nannies.' He did not want to share childcare responsibilities and did not respect my career as much as I needed him to do. So, I took the difficult decision that I needed to end that marriage.* **Ann Francke**

For **Bridget**, the right partner means someone who respects her, works as a team to care for their kids, works hard to achieve their shared goals and who challenges her to be her best.

> *He doesn't judge me as a woman; he doesn't judge me as Māori. I don't judge him as being Tongan or being a male. We have very similar upbringings and morals. He grew up in Mangere, so the warring neighbours, and we still to this day tease each other about which suburb is best I know that he brings skills to this business that I have no idea about and I would not be in the position that I'm in right now if it wasn't for his skills and what he gives freely to not just help me as a woman, as his wife, as the mother of his children, but also what he gives me to advance myself just as a human.* **Bridget Foliaki-Davis**

If you are new to a relationship, set the expectations for shared housework at the beginning. Patterns start early and are hard to shake later on. 'Playing house' is very tempting but can have a lasting negative impact on your relationship in the long run. What may be just a kind act of love in ironing his shirts now may become a bitter source of resentment later.

Again, at the beginning of a relationship agree on priorities and bottom lines. Often one partner does not care as much about whether the cushions on the sofa are neatly arrangement as the other. One partner's clean house is the others squalor. Agree a timetable as well, not only who will do what, but when and how often.

> *I think it's about setting out clear guidelines and priorities with your partner or your support system. This is one that's not going be solved overnight. I always encourage young women who are just entering a serious relationship or are getting married, have the discussion up front, 'How do we want to live?' Talk about careers and talk about children.* **Brenda Trenowden**

I did this with my partner at the beginning of the relationship. We decided that two medium sized careers (one for us each) would be best, rather than one stellar career at the expense of the other. We have alternated our roles so that neither of us had a full on job at the same time. For example, when I was CE of the Ministry for Women, my partner worked on his PhD and had the flexibility our family needed. I also made a mess of ironing his work shirts the first time I volunteered to help and since then have not been 'allowed' to iron. Such a shame.

For many of us, we are in mature relationships and don't now have the opportunity the beginning of a relationship brings to set out shared expectations. For us, we have to work through what can be a tough re-negotiation of long standing implicit agreements. What can work is keeping a log together on what you each do around the house. Lots of what you may do is invisible to your partner and by quantifying it you can start a rational, objective conversation about what each of you do and how much.

For many of us, there isn't a partner to share the work with. For those parenting alone, happily solo or still looking for the right partner, having the right community and support structures around you is critical. Increasingly women are choosing to enlist the help of extended family, with multiple generations living together, much like we have done for centuries or creating communities of friends who look out for each other and share resources.

CHALLENGE THE MYTHS

We are not islands. Our relationships are impacted by the social and cultural expectations around us and we bring into our relationships programming about gender roles.

> *Subconsciously, we can put ourselves into self-limiting boxes. We tell ourselves we can "only be this" or we "will never be able to achieve that." There is power in consciously examining the internal stories we have been taught. Our power begins the moment we decide to embrace our potential."* **Alexia Hilbertidou**

As women we often end up holding this myth: If I don't do it, it won't get done. Or it won't get done properly. We mistrust others to work to our standards or to do things the way we do them. We assume we are better at doing housework or looking after others. There is no evidence to suggest that women are better at cleaning loos than men. We can challenge our own assumptions. So the next time someone does something around the house, do not re-do it your way or growl up them for not doing it 'right'.

Another myth is that having a tidy house and organising others (outer peace) will make our insides better (inner peace). I have fallen prey to this myth. If I just tidy everything up, I will feel better, and more in control and then I can relax and will be happy. But of course, it is only an illusion or temporary (the wet towels seem to end up on the floor only seconds after they have been picked up).

Check in with yourself, what are you really trying to achieve by taking the emotional load of your family or workplace? Ask yourself am I really going to tidy and shop my way to happiness? Are you attaching your sense of peace and wellbeing to the state of your floors? If so, are you okay with that?

KEEP TALKING

As we all know, relationships aren't static, things keep changing on and around us. So, if you have checked your behaviours and re-negotiated the chores, you are going to need to keep talking about it and checking in.

> *Although in any relationship, things change. You have children - things change. You have a different job, things change. By open communication you can negotiate what works for each other, and I realise that getting back to what a feeling is, the real raw feeling, is quite helpful. 'I'm tired or I just want you to listen, I don't need you to tell me what to do.' Those kind of things. Getting back to really raw, honest communication saves time.* **Stacey Morrison**

I found that during parental leave, I ended up doing pretty much all the housework. Where before babies, he might have done the groceries; I now did. But when I went back to work, the housework load didn't automatically shift back. So it is all about negotiation and re-negotiation. It's kind of like a packet of chocolate biscuits with caramel centres, you eat one and then all of sudden there is none left in the packet: you buy everyone's Christmas presents one year, then all of sudden two decades later you realise that that is madness.

YOU CAN'T BE RESPONSIBLE FOR OTHER PEOPLE'S FEELINGS

The weight that comes with emotional labour can be very tiring and stressful. We assume the responsibility for making sure everyone around us is healthy and happy. But in doing so, we often end up absorbing other's pain and unhappiness, all without social work or counselling training.

Jackie shares with us what she has learnt through working with women in abusive relationships about how to reduce the personal toil that supporting others brings.

> *It's about boundaries. If you've got all the energy in the world for it, at that particular moment, do it. It's fine. But also, be aware of that really unhealthy dynamic that occurs when you are taking on other people's shit. I learnt this through my marriage. He made me responsible for all his feelings. Everything was my fault. So, if things were bad, that was my fault.*

> *I'm now very good with emotional boundaries. I say to women, your dilemma is not my dilemma. I work with women who are in very traumatic circumstances. What I've learnt is that if people are in shit soup, you can't fix them. This is one of my big sayings – you can't save people; you can only love them. If you're in shit soup, I can't pull you out. You've got to pull yourself out of shit soup. It's not my responsibility to do that.*

> *Empathy is not about being kind. Empathy is when you take something from somebody and then you give it back to them. You don't hold on to it.*

Women often mistake niceness and kindness to being empathetic, to being a good person. If you're taking on other people's shit (…)then good luck to you sweetheart. But if you take on somebody's shit, and you look at it and you hold it for them while they're dealing with something else and then give it back to them, that's a different thing entirely. **Jackie Clarke**

WHO ARE YOUR TRYING TO IMPRESS?

It was a hard lesson for me, this one. I tried to work in a senior leadership role, parent two young kids, and have a house that was tidy, bake bikkies and always wrap presents with matching paper and ribbon. Not surprisingly I ended up in bed, exhausted, wondering what had to go. It couldn't be the kids and I loved my job (and we needed the money to pay the mortgage anyway). So, it had to be my standards. It felt like I was letting the side down. I hated that someone might pop around (like the Queen? What was I thinking?) and see piles of washing on the lounge floor and dishes overflowing in the sink.

The Queen is never coming to my house, real friends don't care and all those photos of houses in magazines and on Insta are staged. All their junk is hidden in the garage or under their beds until after the photographer has gone. Bet you can't open any of their cupboards without crap falling out because it has been stuffed in there for the shoot.

This is something I've had to learn (…) most ambitious people want to do everything really well and so you put the same kind of high expectations on everything at home (…) your children, how your house looks, and your meals (…) everything.

It comes back to priorities. If we don't have the healthiest meal every night, I can live with that, (…) because it's more important to have some nice time with the family. It may be that right now your job needs to be prioritised, you may have to accept that your house is not always going be perfect or that sometimes your kids are going go to school and they're not going with the cleanest clothes. But, if they go to bed at night happy having had some quality time with you, that's the important thing.

Women can be the worst judges of other women. I've felt some hard looks at the school gate, as a working mum, because I'm barely ever there and when I am, I sometimes feel like I'm being judges by other women because I'm not at the coffee mornings, I won't be going to the school fete, and I haven't baked a homemade cake. My daughter has learned to bake the cakes herself and sometimes she even bakes them for the other mothers who work. We each need to find the norm that works for us and to be happy with it. **Brenda Trenowden**

Work out what standards matter to you and ignore everything else. For example, sun-dried towels give me pleasure, so I will wash them and hang them on the line, but having a utensil draw that is beautifully laid out, so it looks like it's ready for a surgeon to operate, isn't something I aspire to.

Work out what you care about. Do nothing else. We have had shabby chic and scandi white as interior design fads. Let's push for had-a-really-long-week chic as the next look. Who's in?

ASK FOR HELP OR, IF YOU CAN, BUY HELP
Finally, one of things I found was that not only did I feel like I needed to have a perfect house, but I also felt I had to do it all myself. Asking for help, or even paying for help, felt like showing weakness. If you have these thoughts, please stop. No one dies wishing they had cleaned soap scum off the shower more.

> *I used help and I would encourage people to do that, but do it in a savvy way. Use help, as much help as you can afford, whether that's relatives or whether it's au pairs. Actually, just get over the fact that you're not going to have a perfect home. Okay, so there are dishes in the sink, or there are crumbs on the counter, or sometimes there's laundry that's not done. It's not the end of the world.*
>
> *Obviously, nobody wants to live in a hovel but just relaxing the standards of perfection and thinking, 'Yeah, it's okay sometimes.' Just like sometimes you need a duvet day, sometimes we leave dishes in the sink; get over it.* **Ann Francke**

We expect that we can be superwomen. And we are super women. But we can't do everything all at the same time.

Let's help each other
As women we can really help ourselves on this one. While we can be our <u>own</u> worst enemies, we can also be very judgey about others. I remember helping out at a school fair and one mother 'censoring' the baking. The stuff that didn't make her standards went in the bin. Really.

Look at your FB or Instagram posts. Do you push away the dirty dishes to take the perfect dining shot? Do you angle the camera lens so you can't see the washing pile / cat vomit / 10 000 lego pieces? Are you buying into the 'my life is perfect' trope and airbrushing your life? If so, stop. Let's be real about our worlds and proud of who we are. Let's be clear about what we value and the trade-offs we have had to make.

Let's take a stand. Let's not be defined by what the cosmetics and cleaning product companies say makes for a real woman. Let's be defined by what matters most to us.

Let's also make our invisible work more visible. When you can't see emotional labour, it is harder to value. We can do this by sharing what we actually do and valuing the unpaid, unseen work of other women. We can talk about the skills and experience we have gained from this work and be proud of it. We can celebrate our successes (and laugh over our failures).

How To Checklist - Give and Take

- **At the start of a new relationship, negotiate your expectations around sharing house and child-care responsibilities.** If you missed your opportunity, start now by keeping a log of what you both do around the house, and the hours spent. Use this data as the basis of a discussion about workload and tasks. Keep talking and re-negotiating as circumstances change.

- **Don't buy into the myths that a clean house will make you happy – and that you are the only one who can clean it.**

- **Don't take on other people's shit.** Stand alongside them, listen, support them, but don't take responsibility for saving and fixing everything and everyone.

- **Think about what you really care about and focus on that.** Check in with yourself. Are you running yourself ragged trying to impress someone with your clean house, garden, car and kids? Does whoever you are trying to impress give a hoot? Are they even thinking about you?

- **Ask for help and if you are lucky enough to be able to, buy yourself some help.**

- **Don't judge other women's choices.**

- **Don't airbrush your life on social media.** We all know that your house doesn't look like that all the time and we don't care. We like you anyway, regardless

---

Endnotes

1   http://archive.stats.govt.nz/ Census/2006CensusHomePage/QuickStats/quickstats-about-a-subject/unpaid-work/unpaid-work-within-own-household.aspx

2   https://www.theguardian.com/inequality/2018/ feb/17/dirty-secret-why-housework-gender-gap

3   https://www.theguardian.com/inequality/2018/ feb/17/dirty-secret-why-housework-gender-gap

4   Ruppanner, Leah; Branden, Maria and Jani Turunen (2018) Does Unequal Housework Lead to Divorce? Evidence from Sweden Sociology, Vol 52 (1) 75-94

5   https://money.com/women-work-home-gender-gap/

6   https://www.tuc.org.uk/news/tuc-calls-overhaul-shared-parental-leave

7   https://aifs.gov.au/aifs-conference/fathers-and-parental-leave

8   https://aifs.gov.au/media-releases/families-working-together-getting-balance-right

9   Hartley, Gemma (2018) Fed Up. Navigating and Redefining Emotional Labour for Good, Hodder and Stoughton, London

PUT YOUR MASK ON FIRST

– Rachel Petero –

* Set family and emotional boundaries
* Reflect; celebrate the struggle, learn from the joy
* Personalise your selfcare plan, do one thing every day
* Plan for the dips, delete 'I'm busy' from your vocab
* Focus on the now and get out of your head

Selfcare wasn't a word growing up in Avondale, West Auckland. *Westie* was!

Our geographical location stereotyped us as 'westies': mullet haircuts, black T-shirts, and ripped jeans for the guys , and leopard-print fabric, UGG boots, and permed hair for the girls. I definitely had the perm thing going on, and my first boyfriend had a mullet, so I suppose we were 'westies'.

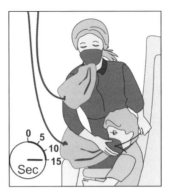

(8.PUT YOUR MASK ON FIRST)

Mental health was for 'mental people' in those days. Those crazy people who talked to themselves or had been locked up in Carrington (a mental health institute in West Auckland). Mental health wasn't talked about and it definitely wasn't cool to talk about issues like depression, anxiety or suicide. I had whānau (family) members locked up at Carrington. None of them have recovered fully.

I don't ever remember hearing about suicide in our whānau, hapū (sub-tribe) or iwi (tribe of related people) growing up. The mask of alcohol and marijuana was prevalent in those days. Now thinking about it … maybe that was the way mental health was hidden.

Mental health has caught me off-guard when I have least expected it. Bouts of depression and self-doubt in times of fear and challenge have crept in and taken control. When I could not function in everyday activities, I knew it was time to get help.

And so – asking for help so you can put *your* mask on first, is step one.

Growing up in our small whānau of four also meant helping out. My sister and I would trip around the Waikato region of the North Island, in the back of dad's green Cortina, to 'work' at tangihanga (funerals), poukai (tribal celebrations of significant tribal people or history) and many celebrations. I emphasise the word 'work' because you never turned up to a marae (meeting place and house for tribal members to gather) just to attend. We had lots of laughs though, at Mangatangi marae and Nga Tai E Rua marae. My memories are mostly of the strong women who kept the marae warm, safe and running efficiently.

These women of my extended whānau were hard working, resilient women. They worked in the market gardens in Pukekohe, they were rousers for sheep shearers, they were drawn into factory jobs like the freezing works and British Paints, where earning minimum wage was something to be proud of. They were activists, leaders, Kiingitanga[11] purists (Māori King movement in tribal region of Waikato), drinkers, smokers, comedians, cultural performers, weavers, cooks, Kaikaranga (woman of status), healers, machinists, artists, aunties, wives, mums and kuia (older woman). That was only the tip of the iceberg of their super powers or mana.

What I learnt growing up around strong Māori women is that they ruled the roost. I don't know of any Māori whānau who didn't have a kuia, a mum, an auntie, a wife, or a female presence in their lives, who was revered or placed on the highest pedestal. There were also those women you were so scared of, you made sure not to make eye contact with et in quiet moments when you were both alone, they were the kindest, most loving, gentle beings on earth.

I often wonder how my ancestors would express their deepest, darkest moments of stress, anxiety, guilt, shame and depression. Or were they so emotionally strong, physically able, and spiritually centred that they didn't experience life the way we do today?

I believe that pre-colonisation, Māori had the equivalent of a PhD in selfcare mastery through mana motuhake. Mana motuhake is to assert independence and authority towards control of your own destiny. We healed ourselves, our communities, our minds, our bodies and our spirits through the knowledge of our connectedness to our natural environment, and helping to restore the physical and spiritual balance in people and place towards a greater purpose.

For me, tuning my own mana motuhake mindset over the last decade has been a healing process of decolonisation and decluttering. It's my selfcare waka (canoe) where I keep people, traditional knowledge, and things that keep me steering my waka in the right direction, and offload anything that is not serving me, my whānau or my purpose.

Both my grandmothers and my mother have been great role models of mana motuhake and I have learnt about selfcare through their worldview. My grandmothers gave me advice that has unconsciously guided me: one said, 'don't have children.' (I know, right? Who says that?) Mere Nutana Taka (nee Paki) said that, and said it often to her granddaughters. I think what she meant is if you have children you better be ready and equipped to take care of them. My role in our whānau is aunty, mentor and coach to our three nieces and three nephews, and I take my aunty role very seriously.

Shirley Ngatono Marshall (nee Flavell) told me to live life to the fullest and encouraged me to travel. She loved hearing from me when I would randomly call her from London. Her phone number is etched in my memory forever. On her passing, I was in the Loire Valley in Southern France with my uncle, her youngest son. I know that I was there at that moment for our mutual selfcare as we mourned her loss, and made the long trek home together.

My mum also knew I would travel. Consequently she passed on to me the biggest selfcare gift a young woman can receive from her mother: she showed me how to trust and believe in myself, and how to set personal boundaries.

On many occasions, my mum has set personal boundaries with individuals (including me), institutions, collectives and family who have stepped over the line of tikanga (traditional practices and protocols) and respect. Sometimes she wouldn't even have to say anything, she'd just give you that look that tells you 'don't go there' or you pick up on that sixth sense that says, 'I'm not happy with you'. Today what I love is that she has fun with her mana motuhake moments, and we often unpack those 'don't go there' moments over a few wines and laugh out loud till our cheeks hurt.

What I am most conscious of today are my own responses to selfcare and self-determination. Mana motuhake mastery is the goal. Every day I do my best to paddle my 'selfcare waka' in the right direction, learning along the way. Every day I consciously give myself a koha (gift) of mana motuhake which includes 3 things I'm grateful for, 2 people I helped and 1 life lesson for the day. How will you prioritise your selfcare in order to care for others? How will you put on your mask first every day?

Lack of selfcare and the costs

While travelling the globe over the years, I've regularly heard the flight attendant say, 'in the event of an emergency, please ensure that you put your mask on first, before assisting children and those in need.' The purpose of that announcement has stuck with me. If we as women don't practice selfcare and do things for ourselves first (like put on our own masks), we will not be able to help others.

COVID-19 has brought unique challenges to how women and young girls cope with the shifting demands of mental, emotional, physical, and spiritual wellbeing. The next wave

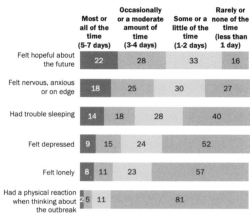

Nearly one-in-five Americans say they have had a physical reaction when thinking about the outbreak

% saying that in the past seven days they have ...

	Most or all of the time (5-7 days)	Occasionally or a moderate amount of time (3-4 days)	Some or a little of the time (1-2 days)	Rarely or none of the time (less than 1 day)
Felt hopeful about the future	22	28	33	16
Felt nervous, anxious or on edge	18	25	30	27
Had trouble sleeping	14	18	28	40
Felt depressed	9	15	24	52
Felt lonely	8	11	23	57
Had a physical reaction when thinking about the outbreak	2 5	11		81

Note: Questions adapted from GAD-7, CES-D, Impact to Event Scale-Revised. Share of respondents who didn't offer an answer not shown.
Source: Survey of U.S. adults conducted March 19-24, 2020.

is likely to be a global 'mental health pandemic'[22] if we don't put our mask on first. In Aotearoa New Zealand, after 23 days of being Covid-19 free, 14 new cases were announced. Although the source could clearly be linked to returning citizens, for those who had rejoiced at beating the virus and dreamed of returning to 'normal' it was a sharp reminder that normal was no longer achievable. The world had changed and the threat was not over.

In these unprecedented times, women have to put their masks on first for protection against disease, depression and death. When women and young girls put their masks on first, we give others permission to do the same.

As we explore some of the costs of mental health, we also start to see the hidden stigmas and stereotypes that prevent women from putting their mask on first.

Survival of the fittest

Recent social neuroscience research talks about modifying emotions and behaviours through 'self-regulation', the process by which people change their thoughts, feelings, or actions to satisfy personal and societies' goals and standards.

Todd F. Heatherton's research further shows a direct link to today's contemporary societal issues faced by women and young girls, such as addiction, depression, anxiety, substance reliance and substance abuse, eating disorders, reoccurring health issues, sleep deprivation and stress related diseases.[3]

In other self-regulation research, Dorothea Orem's *Model of Nursing or Self-Care Nursing Theory*[4], developed between 1959–2001, used in rehabilitation and primary care settings, encourages the patient to be as independent as possible. Dorothy's model of self-regulation excellence is globally recognised.

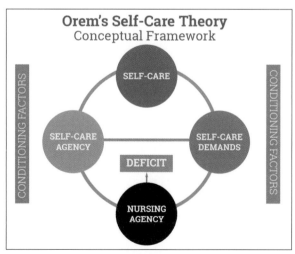

Source: https://nurseslabs.com/dorothea-orems-self-care-theory

A woman's ability to self-regulate and practice self-care of our physical, mental, emotional and spiritual wellbeing is often the last item on our to-do-list. A study done by Michelle Seager, who works largely with women seeking self-care balance, and a leading authority in Sport, Health, Activity Research and Policy (SHARP) gives us insight into motivations of cancer survivors and their behavioural choices to not prioritise exercise, even though it was proven to support their overall wellbeing.

The results showed if people who have faced a life-threatening illness are not able to prioritise their own self-care, which they know firsthand has tangible benefits, then we have a real problem as a society.[5]

Let's take a deeper dive into the challenges faced by young girls and women to prioritise self-care and why survival of the fittest is harder than we think.

Depression and anxiety

According to the World Health Organisation, globally young women report higher rates of depression, self-harm, stress and anxiety than young men, on average.[6] Depression is not only the most common women's mental health problem but may be more persistent in women than men.[7] Approximately 264 million people in the world have experienced depression from the age of 14,[8] and as women are half the world's population, depression and anxiety truly are one of women's greatest miseries. Putting on our masks first, by seeking and asking for help, must be normalised if we are ever going to beat this hidden disease.

Linda Jenkinson spent 25 years abroad, and based on her travels and work in developing countries, she summarises her experience of mental health in the following way:

> *I think a lot of the mental health issue is that people have got into fight and flight, high anxiety, huge amounts of stimulation and challenge.* **Linda Jenkinson**

Mental health factors which specifically affect women (like depression, anxiety and mood disorders) are not impacting men at the same rate as women.[9] This is not to say that men and young boys do not suffer from mental health issues. However, what the research and evidence is saying is that there are additional and specific gender dynamics that lead to higher rates of mental illness in women.

Major life transitions (like pregnancy, motherhood and menopause) can create physical and emotional stress. Negative life experiences (like infertility and perinatal loss, poverty, sexism, discrimination, domestic violence, gender bias in the workplace and isolation in leadership and board roles) also impact on women's mental health and wellbeing.[10]

Today, there is less stigma involved in taking 'mental health days'. These days are now more commonly used as part of a personal selfcare regime. Anjum fully expects to have mental health days off work to rest and recover as the founder of an NGO.

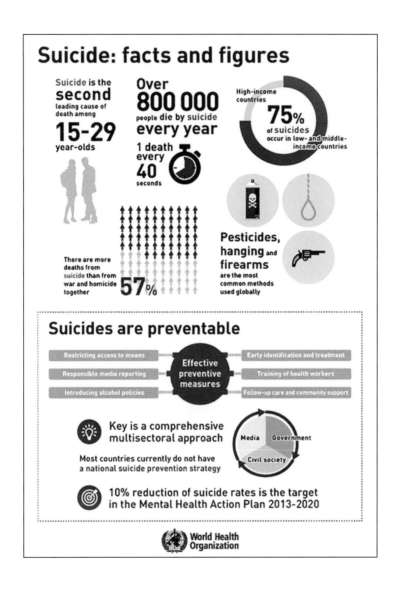

Yep. On average, I expect to take around six mental health days a year, where I literally just sleep all day. I sleep till two or three because I'm that exhausted, cos I've just been running around and doing this and that and the other, and it's just like my body's telling me to just stop work. **Anjum Rahman**

Understanding that there are additional and different mental health challenges for women and men will help government, society, and workplaces provide different masks for different needs.

The emotional downward spiral
COVID-19 crisis

COVID-19 has been a mental health pandemic of epic proportions. Lockdown has led to spikes in remote support care services for mental health sufferers, and the emotional downward spiral for women and children seeking shelter from physical partner violence under lockdown. Women's Refuge in NZ reported a 60 percent increase of their services during lockdown with China also recording nearly double the usual volume of family violence and police callouts in one city alone.

With an impending global mental health pandemic because of COVID-19,[11] studies show women make up 60 per cent of employees entering the US healthcare industry.[12] Health workers are the beating heart of every health system and the majority (70 percent) are women, according to the World Health Organisations report, *Delivered by Women, Led by Men*.[13]

The tragic news of Dr Lorna Breen, a top emergency room doctor at a Manhattan hospital, who committed suicide after working directly with COVID-19 patients, is a reminder of the emotional burden healthcare workers face while battling COVID-19.[14] When women like Dr Breen (and 800,000 people worldwide) lose their lives to suicide annually, is this not enough for us all to stop and make a radical change in how we treat all forms of mental health?[15]

Mental health can also start early in life. Kristen shares courageously about her mental and emotional health challenges as a young child.

> *"For me, as a kid, I tried to take my life three times because for me I thought I was the worst kid in the world, and I couldn't stop myself […] Again, living two lives as a child and having to participate as that of the opposite sex to which I was physically born. I had to simulate that, deal with the anxieties, and I just thought I was doing something totally wrong and letting down my family, and all those other things. But in the end it was society letting me down".* **Kristen Worley**

Globally women of all ages, sexuality, race, profession and backgrounds, just like Dr Lorna Breen and Kristen, are learning to cope or face the COVID-19 crisis of mental health.

In the UK, women are taking on greater levels of stress and anxiety during the country's lockdown with six out of 10 women (61%) finding it harder to stay positive day-to-day, compared with 47% of men, and women are bearing the brunt of the emotional and financial fall out too. Across Australia, Canada and the US the statistics are consistent showing that women are more likely to experience negative mental health impacts than men with loneliness, restlessness and depression recording consistently higher than men by an average of 8 to 10%.

Radical change globally is required for the government to setup alternative health systems, policies and programmes to break down the barriers of mental illness, As we support more women to step out from the COVID-19 crisis of mental health, through more robust support services, policies and addressing societal stigma we start to heal and learn.

Physical self-harm

Globally, the World Health Organisation stats paint a grim picture of women's physical self-harm. Women are more sleep deprived, physically malnourished and are using alcohol and drugs to manage our mental and physical wellbeing.[16]

Alcohol is the most commonly used substance by girls and women, and women abuse prescription drugs more often than menaccording to Canada's Womens Health Matters.[17] The lifetime prevalence rate for alcohol dependence (another commonform of self-harm) disorder) is more than twice as high in men thanalso higher for women according to WHO. In developed countries, approximately one in five men and one in 12 women will develop alcohol dependence during their lives.[18]

The dependency of drugs, alcohol and substances to cope can have lifetime effects across all areas of a women's home and work environments. How government and society tackle the economic and social responsibility of this physical mental illness is the Trillion Dollar economic question.

The lifetime effects of physical eating disorders for girls and women with AN (anorexia nervosa) and BN (bulimia nervosa) is staggering. Eating disorders have the highest mortality rate of any mental illness. A study by the National Association of Anorexia Nervosa and Associated Disorders (ANAD) reported the following eating disorder statistics:

- **10 million American women suffer from eating disorders.**

- **In the UK it is estimated that 1.8 million women have a eating disorder**

- **Approximately 15% of Australian women experience an eating disorder during their lifetime**

In 2016 Anorexia was one of the leading killers of Kiwi teenage girls and the third most common chronic illness for young women, behind obesity and asthma. Just over 1088 diagnoses were recorded in 2015, up 50% from 2011.

The evidencecost to young girls and women is high when education about self-care, self-regulation and self-determination is not the norm. Mental health once identified is treatable when caught in time. The signs of and cost of women suffering physical self-harm, may be more evident than emotional, and mental illness is society's mask of public shame to bear.and as we did during COVID-19 we all need to look out, pop over or just notice our neighbours, families and friends.

Economic impact

There is a social impact mental, emotional impact cost to women as evidenced above and then there is an economic and productivity cost. The impact of mental health to society also impacts our global economy, which loses approximately US$ 1 trillion per year in productivity due to depression and anxiety.[19]

In the workplace, 61 percent of working women felt that workplace wellness programmes needed to better address the specific needs of each gender, and working women reported being more stressed than men, according to the *2019 Cigna 360 Wellbeing Survey*.[20]

As corporates, governments and communities get busy working out what this means in practice, in policy, and in life in general, all these diverse groups of women need to be mentally, emotionally, spiritually and physically strong enough to put their masks on first.

In the UK, poor mental health is estimated to carry an economic and social cost of £105 billion a year in England alone.[21] An extensive report, focused on evidence and the voice of women, clearly showed that rates of mental illness are rising faster in women than men. A taskforce has been setup to address gender-based violence and trauma for women of all diversities.[22]

In her UK workplace, Ann comments:

> *I have a gender balanced executive team where the men and the women can be themselves, and we all work flexibly, and we look after our mental health. We pay it forward to our people and we don't tolerate politics. We have robust, honest, authentic discussions and we make good decisions most of the time because we give ourselves that space, and we have a great relationship with our board because we're transparent. Through difficult times and challenging times, we support each other.*
> **Ann Francke**

New Zealand's first wellbeing budget was launched in May 2019. It is a step forward in improving the state of our environment, the strength of our communities, and the performance of our economy. This collaborative and evidence-based approach to wellbeing for all New Zealanders includes $495 million for new mental health service programmes and suicide prevention.[23]

New Zealand women were around 1.6 times more likely to have been diagnosed with a common mental disorder (20 perccent) than men (13 percent), and rates were higher in all age groups. The highest rate for women was from 35–44 years of age (23.8 percent) and for men was from 45–55 years of age (15.5 percent).[24]

One in five New Zealanders experience mental health or addiction challenges at any given time. All this comes at huge social cost to individuals and families, and to the economy. It's estimated that in 2014 the economic cost of serious mental illness alone was NZ$12 billion, or five percent of GDP.[25]

How to put your mask on first

Are you the woman who gives, gives, gives till you have nothing more to give? Today needs to be different. Stop, take a breath and put your mask on first. Today I challenge you to stop everything and read this part of the chapter for no other reason than you need to do something for only you.

Until you put your mask on first, nothing changes. The women in this chapter have been where you are. Read what they did and find something that works for you.

Let's find out what selfcare works for our 14 amazing women

Setup emotional boundaries

In preparing this chapter, I noticed how the women we interviewed purposefully integrated whānau into their selfcare plans. They also knew when to take time out for self. Could this be the 'mask' or the key to achieving the balance we are seeking as women?

Setting clear emotional boundaries, like tikanga (protocols) in my culture, preserve our traditions and genealogy. These boundaries are in place to keep ourselves and our families safe.

Let's look at an example of how women do this in reality

Stacey is a mum of three tamariki (children) and has a pretty hectic schedule across her radio, television and Te Reo Māori language revitalisation contracts.

> *I've been shit at it before. I realised that I'm really good at doing it for other people and I'm not so good at doing it for myself. I've even thought about being an agent, because I'm so good at [doing] it for others. Then I realised actually I need an agent for me, and she's awesome. This is where I work with my agent to weigh up the cost based on the results, and decide if that contract is worthwhile. So yeah, I got to that place. I am also very mindful of the things that I can do for aroha, as a result of doing my paid jobs.* **Stacey Morrison**

Stacey and her husband Scottie are great role models for Māori parents and rangatahi as they develop Te Reo Māori and Māori knowledge in every part of their personal and professional careers.

Bridget is building a whānau or family business with her husband, to leave to their three children. She talks about making a critical decision to say enough is enough, to set boundaries for selfcare and safety, that changed their business and lives forever.

It got to [such] a tipping point with both of us (Mahei even more so than me), that I said to him, 'Love, we can't continue to operate like this, because the more that we give, the less that we're actually putting into our own immediate requirements.'[...]So we made a conscious decision. I'm going back [to] probably 2010, maybe, when we both sat down and went, 'Enough is enough. We can't continue to do this,' because the majority of our working week was taken up working on things that were feel-good, but we were living on chicken and rice, and we weren't progressing our family. **Bridget Foliaki-Davis**

Anjum talks about the emotional boundaries our mind can play on us:

Maybe not first. It's okay to sometimes not put yourself first. But it's more just about being kind to yourself really and just trying to put a brake on those negative voices in your head. It's the technique that I was told. So when that negative thinking is going, just start saying the opposite. 'Oh you're so stupid, you're so stupid,' but it's [the negative] voices that are saying it, and you're going, 'I'm not stupid, I'm a smart person. I can do this, I can do that. I am not stupid.' Just say it. **Anjum Rahman**

Our dynamic millennials, **Arizona** and **Alexia**, have the full support of their whānau and especially their mums, who clearly taught them to put boundaries in place to keep them safe in different environments.

Once I got [to] Epsom Girls Grammar, and then somehow by God's grace got trusted to be the Head Girl in 2013, all of those mini experiences that my mother [and] my grandmother had put us through growing up, they came to the forefront once I got that leadership role. Because all of a sudden, I was in a space of influence in front of people who didn't look like me, sound like me, think like me. Had I not had that upbringing, in the time where I actually needed to fend for myself, I would have folded straight away. Because I didn't understand the responsibility, [what] it meant to now represent the few little kids in the corner at school in assemblies that did look like me, sound like me, talk like me. **Arizona Leger**

Being Greek and part-Samoan, whanau is really important to me. After years of me working unpaid on a shoe-string budget, I am thankful that now I can hire inspirational women in my whanau to work with me at GirlBoss New Zealand. It is so motivating for me as a daughter, as a niece, to see my Aunty and Mum working at GirlBoss NZ for a cause they are so passionate about. My mum and Aunty both have worked hard in so many jobs for many years, so now to see them working in a job they love so much, earning above the living wage, and waking up every day with passion and purpose for our mission, it's a really special part of being an entrepreneur. Success to me is uplifting those around me, to help them to succeed. I have always been taught that there is enough sun for everybody. **Alexia Hilbertidou**

Royal is teaching her daughter what the reality of work looks like in the twenty-first century, and what not to put up with when she finally gets to that point in her life.

> *I block out on my work diary first thing in the morning. I used to be proud to be able to be in the office quite early, to work with my team to empower them. But instead I use that to do some exercise with a trainer or myself, to empower myself. [...] Most importantly, I also now diarise times for social dates with friends; with my husband, with my parents, with my kids. I block out the long weekends, [...] to really just do something that's good for my soul. It's not actually for anyone else - it's just for me to feel happy that I am doing something that actually gives a sense of satisfaction to my heart.* **Royal Reed**

Traci talks about staying in the middle space and being 'in flow', which means choosing what is important and what isn't in the moment, and once you've made that decision letting the rest flow from there.

> *"Take care of the kaupapa and the kaupapa will take care of you" is one of her biggest life lessons. Being physically and emotionally fit is important because that gives me a good, solid base. I'm clear that I have only so much time on Earth, and I want to spend it with people and in roles that are positive, affirming and uplifting. I trust my whaanau and friends to keep me on track and to affirm and love me, even when I can't love myself. And in return, I provide that same support for them.* **Traci Houpapa**

Reflect on the last year

To start off, reflect on the last year. Give yourself time to celebrate what went well, what didn't go so well, and what you might do differently moving forward. Let this year be the year for your mask to be put on first.

Your mask is your selfcare. It is something you need every day. Choose one or two of your daily tasks to focus on. If putting yourself first or prioritising yourself is new for you, here are a few examples:

Selfcare could be taking an uninterrupted shower or bath at 10pm when the kids are asleep, while your partner or flatmate does the late night washing load and makes the lunches for the kids. Instead of doing everything, you are now enrolling others' support.

Selfcare could be writing a text to yourself every night or morning saying to yourself, 'You got this. You rock. You are loved.' And sending a text to one friend every day.

A great suggestion is to use a digital device, get a diary or journal, and use it to keep a log of your selfcare practices. Plan and schedule small changes into your diary or calendar, and set reminders for yourself. Edith shares her practice.

Daily reflection, diaries or journaling is useful too – as a way to think back on what you did. I kept a lot of journals growing up. Some of my most favourite objects are journals I kept with friends, or my own journals. **Edith Amituanai**

Make a list of the things you do every day that bring you joy and good energy like prayer, running, walking, meditation, reading and writing. If areas or people in your life are de-energising it could be a sign to reassess a situation or relationship. Edith also encourages women to focus on what comes naturally.

I'm a big strength-based approach kind of girl, so always play your strengths, but how do you know your strengths? They appear naturally, I think. I'm a forceful girl. What I've realised is that our strengths appear naturally, I think. I think acknowledging what came naturally to you, what you enjoyed doing. You might have felt so free - being free is a good way to describe something for me. Did you feel free doing that or did you feel excited by doing that? That's a useful way to recognise some of the things that you're possibly born to do. **Edith Amituanai**

If you have noticed that your mental, physical, spiritual or emotional health are not where you want them to be, then we hope there is something new to try in this chapter. Decide which everyday practices work for you.

Now it's time to explore and find out what else you can add to your selfcare kete (basket).

Arizona reflects on where she was and where she's heading.

Probably a year ago, selfcare in the way that I knew it to be (like, my selfcare) was terrible because I was just going straight from work to whatever the voluntary space is after, [and] back to work again. And it was not something that I think is considered, from a female context, because for maybe male (I don't know research on this), but for maybe male it's that nine to five, switch off, go home, do whatever it is, and that's their selfcare time, right? So naturally as a CEO or as a decision maker who's a male, you're sitting there going, well you should get your selfcare time in the five to nine. **Arizona Leger**

Before you jump into your self-care planning and get on with the doing, take some thinking time out to pause, breath and reflect. Kristen shares how she recalibrates.

I do some meditation. I do a lot of reading and illustration. […] I do a lot of reflection and it helps me to recalibrate and spend time tramping in the wilderness with my dog, it helps me to go two steps forward one step back, recalibrate. Two more steps forward and keep going. That's how I kind of work I recalibrate. It's funny cos people always ask me, in terms of the successes I've had, it's been a long journey to get there and lots of pressure put on me 'mafia oppression top down power approach' by global sport leadership and government trying to stop me at all cost to prevent me

from bring forward the truth and change. Their tactics only fired up my commitment, my calling and I could not stop it anyway even if I wanted too. It's always about self-assessment, and rethinking, continued learning, and trying to look at doing things differently. One person can make change if they have the will and commitment.
Kristen Worley

It sounds obvious but not many of us stop to ask ourselves how it all went? We are so busy 'in' our lives we never step out to work 'on' our lives. I've learnt this in business.

Working 'on' your business is different to working 'in' your business. You need to constantly come out of working 'in' your business/ life/ career to see the bigger picture, to give you context, and see the situation from a different perspective.

Jackie always brings a new perspective, and when asked about women constantly running on empty through lack of selfcare, she shares honestly:

"Stop that shit. Simply stop it. I've seen it and I do it, I've done it. I don't give a fuck anymore. I'm like, you bastards, I get paid $54,000 a year before tax plus another $9,500 for car related costs. So, I get paid $54,000. I'm not paid enough to run around like a headless chook, but also it's not good for me. Now what I do, is I'm working more from home, obviously, but I do yoga twice a week now. He comes to my house. I'm like, 'fucken bring it on.' It's an hour and a half, and that's fantastic." **Jackie Clark**

Take time out to look at your life, career and business on a regular basis. You can do this with others as well as doing a self-review. It's a great way to check-in and stay accountable to yourself and others.

A few questions to start you off:

- What / Who brought value to your life in the last 12 months?
- What / Who brought joy and energy to your life in the last 12 months?
- What / Who de-energised you in the last 12 months?
- What / Who will you be taking forward into the next 12 months?
- What / Who will you let go of in order to move forward in the next 12 months?

As a result of your review, what are your top three lessons? (add more if you want to).

Celebrate the struggles, learn from the joy

So now you have a baseline of where you are. Keep it and check in again, as and when you need to. It's great to look back after a year from the date you started and see what's changed.

How will you celebrate and do things differently this year? It's a question I get a few blank stares in response to. Women in particular find this question difficult to answer. Mostly because we don't celebrate enough. We typically get busy in our careers, life and business, and forget to notice all the millimetre steps it took, all the people who supported one project, one event, one new hire, one workshop, one new baby, one new client. Normalising and talking through the struggle, celebrating when we fall, fail or falter, creates an environment where it's okay to make mistakes and where we're encouraged to embrace an opportunity to learn something.

Celebrate your progress rather than only focusing on the final destination.

I love how **Stacey** celebrates moments of selfcare.

> *I am drawn to things like yoga, meditation, karakia – those kind of things are really important for me. Then when I take mindful moments, tiny mindful moments (like the total win of being able to have a bath by yourself that's candlelit), I'm sure to tell myself, 'This is me time' and I affirm it to myself. I go, 'This is your time. Use all your senses. Smell it, look at it, feel it.' I actually tell myself this. 'Here you are recharging', so that I'm really present in what I'm doing there. Yoga and those kinds of things, I'm not in a good practice right now, but even yoga nidra, which is maybe 20 minutes of deep meditation and relaxation, helps me a lot. Things like magnesium helps me calmness-wise, and I have to keep an eye on iron, all those kinds of things, so that's on a physical level. Those are things that I've realised for me I have to be mindful of.*
> **Stacey Morrison**

Celebration can be treating yourself to an extra hour lie-in on the weekend. A lunch with the girls. A day of no chores, no housework and no washing! A Netflix night in. Or go all out with a capital D for Decadence.

Arizona talked passionately about her superhero mum and how much she deserves selfcare.

> *Obviously good selfcare (looking like massages and all that type of stuff) it's literally [where] if my mum got a day to herself, I would happily leave her alone.*
> **Arizona Leger**

It can also be a text to your manager for a job well done. It could be a walk, a prayer, writing down what you are grateful for, it could be a public post to acknowledge someone, a team, or delivery of a recent programme or event. It could be a phone call to your business partner for securing a new client and/or contract. It could also be certificates, shouting your team lunch, a weekend away, vouchers, bonuses… whatever works. Peer recognition in an authentic and fair way is always something I feel we don't do enough of, yet it is one of the easiest ways we can celebrate success and the joy of others.

As mums, women in community, leaders and owners of businesses, recognition done well will support you to build engaged, high performing happy teams, communities and ultimately a happier, healthier you!

Alexia makes sure to give herself a break and not set expectations of selfcare too high.

The key is to acknowledge what you have noticed throughout your journey. This includes the struggle as well as the joy.

► *It takes 21 Days to create a Habit*
► *It takes 90 Days to create a Lifestyle*

WHY NOT START **TODAY?**

Personalise your selfcare plan
Everyone needs different things from a selfcare plan.

I love how **Stacey** talks about selfcare from a Māori worldview.

> *I guess it's how we treat others. What's the tikanga of our (Māori) culture and what does it tell us to do? You know, when we say in Māori, 'don't turn up with just your forehead'. Are we following our own tikanga? That's where I think the frameworks and the protocols for our culture are a really good reference. It's about reciprocity and that can come in different forms. If you know that you're not being valued and that you always end up doing that mahi, everyone just expects you to do it, and then they criticise how you do it, and then they throw stones when you do it, then, yep, you've got to make a call. It's really hard, because you can't be unrelated to people [laughs] when you're related. That's a challenge. Sometimes it's about resetting and going, 'Right, okay.' My sister says a good thing. She says when people show you who they are, believe them. So if people actually take you for granted and don't respect you enough, you just need to be your own monitor of, 'okay, that's probably enough'.*
> **Stacey Morrison**

Now it's time to look forward a week, a month or a year from now. Choose a timeframe.

What are three actions you can do now, outside of your comfort zone, to shift you one step closer, from where you are today, to where you ultimately want to be.

If you want to be less stressed and more present with your whānau, taking on more projects at work won't get you to your intention. A more suitable action might be – I am committing to not take on any new projects for the next month, by letting my manager know why, and reprioritising my evenings so that we have 30 minutes of family time without TV, devices or digital platforms to talk and share what we did each day.

Check your actions with a trusted friend, your whānau, a coach or mentor. When you read your actions out loud do they create energy and motivate you to move forward? Do they create excitement and joy within you? If you are not feeling it then they probably need tweaking. Amp up your actions. Does your heart sing when you read your actions aloud? If not, keep refining them until they make you want to dance, and sing from the rooftops.

Strong leadership from organisations, institutions and employers to provide support programmes for mental and emotional wellbeing are antidotes for eradicating mental health issues.

Once you have more clarity you can bring everything together in a selfcare plan. This is a reminder of what you have committed to as short, medium and long term goals for yourself – preferably on one page.

Bridget and her husband Mahei are on a selfcare hack journey and they have a plan.

> *Rather than taking our time, we're trying to hack our way through this business so that we can be in a position [where] we're looking after ourselves and our family and our extended family, but then we can start to give back to our community and to our hapū and our iwi.* **Bridget Foliaki-Davis**

At the start of putting selfcare into practice make sure your plan is visible in your everyday life: your screensaver on your phone on your computer, on your mirror in the bedroom, in the bathroom, in your office. Bridget's selfcare partner is right there by her side every day as a reminder.

> *It's a partnership that I think works because there's that respect. I respect what he gives. It blows me away how hard he works. I'll be fast asleep and he'll be finishing work […] downstairs in our office. He'll come back up to bed at four or five o'clock in the morning and he'll be up again at nine o'clock and he'll be back into it. Then he'll be making sure the kids get to the different things they have to attend, and helping me, or he'll just be out there sweeping the floor, doing whatever is needed to run the household, run the business and also just be an amazing husband. I'm very lucky, but I also like to think I chose wisely!* **Bridget Foliaki-Davis**

Visual references and metaphors will further support you to achieve your goals and support your mindset to focus on what you need, versus a wandering mind which has no focus or direction to your final destination.

According to a recent Accenture report, leaders of corporations play a key role in opening up conversations about mental health challenges. Talking about mental health in the workplace gives permission to employees and employers to do the same.

Do one thing every day for 30 days

Changing habits is a big part of putting your mask on first. For too long women have put masks on for everyone else before themselves. Now it's time to change that habit. It can take seconds or years to form new habits. The point of doing one thing every day for 30 days is to get into a pattern of repetition, that supports new behaviours and actions, that help you take one step forward every day until you are on automatic pilot. Then you try something else, and soon you are a habit changing machine.

Shifting old habits that don't serve you, and creating new ones, will be linked to emotional life experiences. The experts say it takes 21 days to form a new habit. In my experience, whether it takes seconds or years depends on how deep-seated the emotion is and the experience it is related to.

> *It's like choosing an instrument and it takes practice. You have to keep training yourself to get better and better and better at it so it becomes more natural. It becomes more secondary to you in your day-to-day work and then you can move on to the next step. You have to build the infrastructure and the platform to get to those steps. Initially you do it to it to fit in and for safety. Now being on the other side, it is empowering and a tool of change for a better world and a place of leadership. I am no longer hiding, I have found my truthself and my role, my calling to bring global change through the outreach of sport."*
> **Kristen Worley**

For example, putting your hand on a hot stove or touching a live electrical wire will give you an intense and immediate pain or shock. The experience may only take a split second, but for the rest of your life you will have developed the habit of not putting your hand on hot stoves, or touching live electrical wires. The habit will have been formed instantly and permanently.

I look forward to my walks up Maungawhau mountain. I have my clothes ready to change into as soon as I hear the alarm go off. I jump out of bed straight away, and don't have time to hit snooze button.

Practice doing one selfcare task every day for at least 30 days. If it's meditation for five minutes every morning before work, put a plan in place to ensure you do it every day. After 30 days, it will become automatic, and then you can then set your next goal.

Remember to journal the process of how you are feeling, what you are noticing, any lessons learnt, and what new awareness you are creating every day.

Plan for the dips

Visualise everything going really well with your selfcare plan. Then, within a second, an old thought or habit pops back into your head. Or maybe there was an action you weren't able to complete and you find yourself spiralling back into old behaviours? Remember that this is part of the journey of change.

First, give yourself a break. Shake it off. Know that you got this! Your brain wants to take you back to that safe place, that place where everything is comfortable. Those old habits can take time to turn left towards something new, instead of turning right towards the old and familiar.

Imagine you are getting onto a plane and you normally fly coach or economy. It's always been my dream to enter a plane and turn left (towards business class). Your old habit is to turn right when you reach the flight attendant, who checks your seat number. It's the same old, you always fly coach. Deep down, you really want to turn left, but every time you reach the flight attendant, you turn to go left and they say, 'Sorry, you need to turn right. You are flying coach today.' I knew that turning left was going to take time, so I made a plan to one day be able to turn left.

Turning right is your comfort zone, it represents your old habits. It's safe, it's secure, you know the drill. To change your old habit and fly business class, you need to get used to turning left and being stopped by the flight attendant. The flight attendant is life. And life happens. Until one day the flight attendant says to you, 'Welcome aboard, you are in business class. Please turn left and enjoy your flight.' The left represents a new habit being formed. I turned left.

Edith talks about being stuck:

> *It's not selfcare as such that needs to be addressed. It's about acknowledging why you do it and how you do it and when it's appropriate to rest and recharge and all of that. If you don't fix that, I don't see you doing well. I don't see you succeeding, because you just become locked in a cycle.* **Edith Amituanai**

Having a plan for when life happens and you have a dip is a strategy that works for high performance athletes, world leaders and the top percentile of executives and entrepreneurs.

Note down all those old habits, negative self-talk or behaviours that might pop back into your head. Alongside each one, write an antidote for that old habit or behaviour. Having these hacks ready, and planning for those dips in life which are part of the journey of change, is my all-time favourite way to smash through anything that might get in the way of achieving my success.

Delete 'I'm busy' from your vocab

Try counting how many times you say 'I'm busy'. Do you say it to your children? Your partner? Your team? As women wearing multiple hats, we need to be more aware of how and where we spend our time.

It's also important to realise that when we tell ourselves we are busy we are also telling ourselves we are too busy for ourselves and what is important. So it is directly impacting our selfcare.

When someone would ask me 'how is business?' or invite me to something, I started to change how I responded. At the beginning I would say 'yes' to all the invites, especially when I was starting out or when I was setting up in the UK or the Middle East. After a while I had to reassess my boundaries and start to say 'no' to protect my time. Time is our most precious commodity because unlike money, we can't make more of it. It was a good lesson.

I started to change my response and my language when people asked me 'how was business'. I started to practice saying, 'It's in flow, it's productive, the business is on track.' It made a real difference to the conversation. I also replied honestly and could say, 'it's tough at the moment'. It built more trust and my overall relationships grew.

My favourite response when I once asked someone how they were was: 'I'm taking inspired action'.

Take the two words, 'I'm busy', out of your vocabulary and daily conversations, and watch how people respond.

Focus on the now; worrying is a waste of time and energy

Worrying more does not change the outcome of your situation. Think about it. If you worry about the next job promotion, does that change the outcome of getting the job? No. If you get focused on what you can DO to get that next job promotion, one action, one step at a time, your time and energy will lead you towards an outcome.

Worrying about what is not working, what you don't have, what you can't do does not help you to focus on what you can do and what is important to you. We encourage you to spend your time and energy focusing on what you *can* do. It's a total game-changer to help you put on your mask first.

Get out of your head and into your wholeness

You are so much more than your job title, the number of boards you are on, your academic qualifications or your business status. What parts of yourself are yet to be discovered?

Linda is a successful serial entrepreneur who has made million. She recognises her spiritual connection to Indigenous women in Africa. In entering a bi-cultural environment with

Māori, through her role as the UNICEF Aotearoa NZ Chair, she is more aware of the mana or power of connecting with other Indigenous cultures. She shares her spiritual journey of wellbeing and selfcare.

> *I went to Africa to help the world, and I realised it was another form of colonialism, because here am I, a Pākehā chick in the middle of Africa. I realised, as I went through the journey, [that] I was just so happy and so fulfilled… Everyone was like, 'oh they're so lucky because you went and helped them with this.' I said, 'Actually, it's the opposite.' I felt alive again. I felt connected in my heart and in my spirit [-] living like that was so much more rewarding… my experience of having a kaumātua, going onto a marae, feeling that deep connection and being there in that, before you do anything. So it's being. I think that's my biggest thing, is being, and that's really the essence of life. Being in connection; the va; being in relationship as the fundamental juice of life.* **Linda Jenkinson**

As Linda experienced, there is a whole part of ourselves waiting to connect more deeply. Your spiritual connection is part of your wholeness.

Here's a list of some of the personal practices the women we interviewed do regularly.

- **Breathing exercises**
- **Meditation and yoga**
- **Karakia or prayer**
- **Going to church**
- **Working with Indigenous cultures**
- **Working with diverse groups**
- **Journaling and diary writing**
- **Gratitude and affirmations.**

Learning and adopting Indigenous practices is also a great way to put your mask on and support others to do the same.

New Zealand's Dr Mason Durie's *Te Whare Tapa Wha*,[26] an interconnected wellbeing model which recognises the importance of balance and strength of the whole person, encompasses four key principles:

1. **Taha tinana or your physical wellbeing**
2. **Taha wairua or your spiritual wellbeing**
3. **Taha hinengaro or your mental and emotional wellbeing**
4. **Taha whānau or your belonging and wider connection to community, hapū, iwi**

Māori health models like *Te Whare Tapa Wha: Mason Durie*, *Te Wheke: Rose Pere*[27] *Te Pae Mahutonga: Mason Durie*[37] have been integral to shifting New Zealand's approach in health and to the connection of all parts of ourselves.[28]

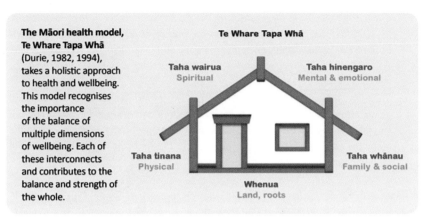

The Māori health model, Te Whare Tapa Whā (Durie, 1982, 1994), takes a holistic approach to health and wellbeing. This model recognises the importance of the balance of multiple dimensions of wellbeing. Each of these interconnects and contributes to the balance and strength of the whole.

Te Whare Tapa Whā

Taha wairua — Spiritual
Taha hinengaro — Mental & emotional
Taha tinana — Physical
Taha whānau — Family & social
Whenua — Land, roots

MODEL OF WHARE TAPA WHA

Rongoa Māori is also a wonderful way to embrace the natural world of traditional wellbeing practices that include the natural environment, using medicinal plants, trees, nature alongside traditional physical connection like massage, prayer or karakia, which are slowly being introduced alongside western clinical practices to improve wellbeing.[29][39]

Share your selfcare plan with other women

Sharing the stories of 14 women in this book has been such an honour. Our hope that we have done justice to their words, their struggles, their successes and their mana. Through their generosity of sharing I have learnt so much about myself and feel like I know them all intimately.

It is through sharing that we normalise topics like mental health, shame, guilt, racism, discrimination, sexism, gender equality, Indigenous practices, Māori values like tikanga (protocols), whānaungatanga (connection), Manaakitanga (kindness), kotahitanga (unity). We start to see a different perspective on the western paradigms of hierarchy versus collectivism.

By sharing, we connect and feel like we see each other in the stories; we are heard, sometimes for the first time; our voices are amplified and have a ripple effect, reaching out our hands to women who have been left behind.

If you only take one thing away from this book, my hope is that you reach out to another women who look different to you, come from a different culture, a different pay band, a different worldview, and let her know, 'You are whole, 100 percent resourceful, and courageous. Everything you want in life is waiting for you just around that next corner.' Then ask her, 'Can I support you to turn that next corner?' And then be silent, hold the space, and be ready for when she is ready.

DONNA KERRIDGE A RONGOA PRACTITIONER   Credit: Tony Dyberg

When you learn that this journey is not about you, it's actually about the next woman, the next generation, the next young girl, you will support her to turn the next corner, and then you are on the right track.

Always remember to have an absolute blast on the journey. Life is too short not to be a gorgeous, powerful, total badass who puts her mask on first in order to support others to do the same.

How To Checklist - Put your mask on first

- **Setup emotional boundaries.** Be courageous, clear and kind with whānau, work colleagues and friends, and let them know what you need in terms of time, support and space to be at your emotional, physical, mental and spiritual best. Find the balance between giving and receiving.

- **Reflect on last year.** Give yourself time to reflect on your last 12 months. Write, journal, video and document what you noticed. Make three lists: what went well, what you can do better, what you want to let go of.

- **Celebrate the struggles, learn from the joy.** Celebrate with people, places and experiences that bring you joy. Notice the steps you have taken every day to move forward and celebrate internally, by being kinder to yourself and externally, by sharing your joy with others. Learn the lessons from your struggles, they can be your greatest gift.

- **Personalise your selfcare plan.** Plan and do three things to take a few more steps (or giant leaps) forward. There is no time like now.

- **Do one thing every day for 30 days.** Choose something new that you can do easily every day as part of your normal routine. This should be simple to implement and should energise you: a gratitude text to yourself every day, a post about something you are passionate about every day, a karakia or prayer every morning or night… whatever you choose, diary it and do it.

- **Plan for the dips.** Plan for those times that are coming where things don't go your way, those roadblocks and down times, and have a plan for how you will cope when they turn up unexpectedly. You will save yourself so much time and energy if you have your hacks ready.

- **Delete 'I'm busy' from your vocab.** Change your mindset by changing your language to more positive, empowering words to keep you moving forward. 'I'm taking inspired action' is my fave.

- **Focus on the now; worrying is a waste of time and energy.** Focus on what you *can* do, what you *do* have and what you *can* control. Use your time and energy to get clear on the outcomes you want to achieve. Your time is valuable, and your energy is best used on what is right in front of you.

- **Get out of your head and into your wholeness.** Embrace all parts of you. Your emotional, physical, spiritual and mental wholeness. Take time to find spaces and people who will support you to explore these areas of who you naturally are, where you came from and where you are going.

- **Share your selfcare plan with other women.** Selfcare and putting your mask on first is so much more fun if you do it with others. Make it fun, be creative, be kind, and be your badass self.

Endnotes

1 https://en.wikipedia.org/wiki/M%C4%81ori_King_
   Movement

2 https://www.globalmed.com/mental-health-is-the-
   next-pandemic/

3 https://www.ncbi.nlm.nih.gov/pmc/articles/
   PMC3056504/#R63

4 https://online.regiscollege.edu/blog/the-pivotal-role-
   of-orems-self-care-deficit-theory/

5 https://www.forbes.com/sites/
   kathycaprino/2015/06/10/why-millions-of-men-and-
   women-find-self-care-so-challenging-and-how-to-
   make-it-easy/#63eb46f27cd9

6 https://www.who.int/news-room/facts-in-pictures/
   detail/mental-health

7 https://www.who.int/mental_health/prevention/
   genderwomen/en/

8 https://www.who.int/news-room/fact-sheets/detail/
   depression

9 https://www.who.int/mental_health/prevention/
   genderwomen/en/

10 https://www.beyondblue.org.au/who-does-it-affect/
   women/factors-affecting-women

11 https://www.globalmed.com/mental-health-is-
   thenext-pandemic/

12 https://www.mckinsey.com/industries/
   healthcaresystems-and-services/our-insights/women-
   in-thehealthcare-industry

13 https://www.who.int/news-room/commentaries/
   detail/female-health-workers-drive-global-health

14 https://www.abc4.com/coronavirus/battling-
   themental-health-crisis-for-medical-workers-on-the-
   frontlines-of-the-covid-19-pandemic/

15 https://wfmh.global/world-mental-health-day-2020/

16 https://www.who.int/mental_health/prevention/
   genderwomen/en/

17 https://www.womenshealthmatters.ca/health-
   centres/mental-health/addiction/prevalence-of-
   womens-substance-abuse/

18 https://www.who.int/mental_health/prevention/
   genderwomen/en/

19 https://www.who.int/news-room/facts-in-pictures/
   detail/mental-health

20 https://wellbeing.cigna.com/360Survey_Report.pdf

21 https://www.gov.uk/government/publications/
   wellbeing-in-mental-health-applying-all-our-health/
   wellbeing-in-mental-health-applying-all-our-health

22 https://assets.publishing.service.gov.uk/government/
   uploads/system/uploads/attachment_data/
   file/765821/The_Womens_Mental_Health_
   Taskforce_-_final_report1.pdf

23 https://treasury.govt.nz/sites/default/files/2019-05/
   b19-wellbeing-budget.pdf

24 https://www.mentalhealth.org.nz/assets/Uploads/
   MHF-Quick-facts-and-stats-FINAL-2016.pdf

25 https://treasury.govt.nz/sites/default/files/2019-05/
   b19-wellbeing-budget.pdf

26 https://www.health.govt.nz/our-work/populations/
   maori-health/maori-health-models/maori-health-
   models-te-whare-tapa-wha

27 https://www.health.govt.nz/system/files/documents/
   pages/maori_health_model_tewheke.pdf

28 https://www.health.govt.nz/our-work/populations/
   maori-health/maori-health-models

29 https://thespinoff.co.nz/atea/27-10-2017/isolation-is-
   making-us-unwell-a-rongoa-maori-perspective/

TAKE
ONE
STEP
FORWARD

We started this book by introducing ourselves and inviting you to join us and 14 other women in conversation. We pointed out that it we don't need fixing at expensive women-in-leadership conferences, but if we are going to get ahead in these tough times we are going to have to work smarter together. All our interviewees have generously shared their secrets in order for you to take your space. Now it's your turn. Decide on one action and take one step forward.

One virtual step forward during COVID19 = #takeyourspace sharing virtually around the world. Let's start a #takeyourspace movement to take one step forward. We need everyone to share 50,000 #takeyourspace hashtags, we need men and women to step forward together.

Get famous people to share! For every famous person sharing #takeyourspace takes 100 steps forward. If women or men of influence like Oprah our very own Jacinda Ardern shares #takeyourspace takes 1,000 steps forward towards Gender equity and equality.

Get your dad's, kaumatua (male elder), kuia (female elder), bosses, bus drivers, brothers, sisters, friends everyone to take one step forward for gender equity. Every step gets us closer to taking our space, our message to an international body like the United Nations to advocate for gender equality and equity.

What you can see, from the insights of the women we interviewed, is that there no one right way to do anything. There is only the way that is right for you. We want you to see what we have shared as a menu to pick from; mix and match and make it right for you.

We want you to see that by taking one step forward or one action, you are changing your course, no matter how small that action is.

Where to from here?

If you were to analyse the actions in this book, you will see some common themes:

Valuing yourself in order to take your unique space means doing the work on yourself. Connect to your whakapapa or genealogy to explore where you come from and why you do what you do. Own your identity, your diversity and tell your story from your space, trust yourself as you take one step forward. You got this, we got you.

Getting in the know might mean working out what you want, but it might also mean understanding your rights or your employer's employment policies. When you have information, you have choices. If in doubt about your first step, look for information that can help you.

Having a plan means getting into action, but thinking through the steps. It's about thinking through your strategy before you ask your boss for a pay rise, or finding people who will support you before you approach them. Often, we act without having thought through the best way of achieving what we are after. Having a plan means we are putting ourselves in the best position to be successful.

Ask for help is easy to say, we know, but hard to do. However the women we interviewed were very clear – they had learnt to ask for help. It is not a sign of weakness or incompetence. Instead it is a key tool. Most people are flattered when you ask them for advice, to be their mentor, or to do something to support you.

Lift up another woman. The message is clear: by helping someone else, we help ourselves. By making space in a meeting, speaking well of a colleague, or encouraging a friend, they will take a step forward and so will we.

If we all take just one step forward, the net effect will be substantial change across the millions of us. If we all ask for pay rises it will be hard to turn us all down. If we all call out inappropriate sexist remarks it will be easier for all of us to do so without stigma, and together we can stamp out all forms of microaggression.

Take one step forward and **Take Your Space.**

Hashtag, follow, tweet, like, share, selfie here's our ask — take a selfie with our book, connect with us on LinkedIn and tag us in any posts with #takeyourspace.

Category	Followers	Number	Value
Influencers	100,000+	1 share	1,000
Famous	10,000+	1 share	500
Connectors	5,000+	1 share	250
Collaborators	1,000+	1 share	100
Community	Under 1,000	1 share	50

TAKE YOU SPACE
CHECKLIST
share how you #takeyourspace on social media

VALUE YOUR WORTH

☐ Check your attitude to money

☐ Focus on what money can do for those you care about

☐ Pay yourself first

☐ Research your worth

☐ Keep an achievement log

☐ Walk in your boss's shoes

☐ Ask

☐ Have a Plan B in case the answer is no

☐ Break taboos about talking about money

LIFT OFF

☐ Be clear about what you want

☐ Make a career plan

☐ Work out who you need on your supporter's team

☐ Fight your negative thoughts

☐ Speak well of other women

TAKE YOUR SPACE

☐ Find your unique space and own it

☐ Say what you mean

☐ Find early adopters Journal and write more

☐ Define your success

☐ Amplify other women's messages

☐ Attract your tribe

☐ Have a 30, 60, 90 day plan

☐ Get comfortable with your physical presence

☐ Invest in support

☐ Trust and believe in yourself

OWN YOUR CONFIDENCE

☐ ABA – always be aware

☐ Be open to alternative worldviews

☐ Practice saying 'no'. It's a full sentence.

☐ Try on your confidence

☐ Tell your story

☐ Face your fears and get uncomfortable

☐ Stop comparing

☐ Help others be confident

MAKE WORK, WORK

- [ ] Work out what work means to you and what you want from your work
- [ ] If you want to work less, work out why it is in your bosses interest
- [ ] Ask for a trial
- [ ] Negotiate new work arrangements based on what you will produce or deliver
- [ ] If you work part-time or flexible hours, do so with pride.
- [ ] Be gentle on yourself

STAND UP FOR YOURSELF

- [ ] Call in your favours
- [ ] Run the marathon not the race Know your rights
- [ ] Support, record and report
- [ ] Get independent professional expert advice
- [ ] Call out and report bad behaviour Own your shine and your s**t
- [ ] Be a forensic investigator Book time off
- [ ] Stepping out is okay too Help others up

GIVE AND TAKE

- [ ] At the start of a new relationship, negotiate your expectations
- [ ] Don't buy into the myths that a clean house will make you happy
- [ ] Don't take on other people's s**t
- [ ] Think about what you really care about
- [ ] Ask for help and if you are lucky enough, buy yourself some help.
- [ ] Don't judge other women's choices.
- [ ] Don't airbrush your life on social media

PUT YOUR MASK ON FIRST

- [ ] Setup emotional boundaries
- [ ] Reflect on last year
- [ ] Celebrate the struggles, learn from joy
- [ ] Personalise your selfcare plan
- [ ] Do one thing every day for 30 days
- [ ] Plan for the dips
- [ ] Delete 'I'm busy' from your vocab
- [ ] Focus on the now; worrying is a waste of time and energy
- [ ] Get out of your head and into your wholeness
- [ ] Share your selfcare plan with other women

NEW ZEALAND SUPPORT

FOR COUNSELLING AND SUPPORT

Lifeline
0800 543 354   (0800 LIFELINE) or free text 4357 (HELP) For counselling and support

Samaritans
0800 726 666   For confidential support for anyone who is lonely or in emotional distress

Depression Helpline
0800 111 757 or free text 4202
To talk to a trained counsellor about how you are feeling or to ask any questions.

Healthline
0800 611 116 For advice from trained registered nurses

Covid-19 Healthline
0800 358 5453
For Covid-19 health advice and inform-ation

www.depression.org.nz
Includes The Journal free online self-help tool.

FOR CHILDREN AND YOUNG PEOPLE

Youthline
0800 376 633, free text 234, email talk@youthline.co.nz or webchat at www.youthline.co.nz (webchat available 7pm – 11pm)
For young people and their parents, whānau and friends.

What's Up
0800 942 8787 (0800 WHATSUP)
(12pm – 11pm Monday to Friday,
and 3pm – 11pm weekends) or webchat at www.whatsup.co.nz
(1pm – 10pm Monday to Friday,
3pm - 10pm weekends) for 5-18 year olds

Kidsline
0800 543 754 (0800 KIDSLINE)
For young people up to 18 years of age.

www.thelowdown.co.nz
Visit the website or free text 5626
For support for young people experiencing depression or anxiety.

www.auntydee.co.nz
A free online tool for anyone who needs help working through problems.

www.sparx.org.nz
An online self-help tool that teaches young people the key skills needed to help combat depression and anxiety.

FOR HELP WITH SPECIFIC ISSUES

0508 Tautoko Suicide Crisis Helpline
0508 828 865
For support if you're in distress, or worried that someone may be at risk of suicide or for those who are grieving a loss.

OUTLine
0800 688 5463 (0800 OUTLINE)
For sexuality or gender identity issues 6pm – 9pm

Alcohol Drug Helpline
0800 787 797, free text 8681
or online chat at alcoholdrughelp.org.nz
For people dealing with alcohol or other drug problems.

He Waka Tapu
0800 439 276 (0800 HEYBRO)
For men who feel they are going to harm a loved one or whanau member.

Women's Refuge Crisis Line
0800 733 843 (0800 REFUGE)
For women living with violence, or in fear, in their relationship or family.

Anxiety Helpline
0800 269 4389   (0800 ANXIETY)

EDANZ
0800 233 269 www.ed.org.nz
For information, support and resources about supporting someone with an eating disorder

Rape Crisis
0800 883 300
For support after rape or sexual assault.

Shakti Crisis Line
0800 742 584   (0800 SHAKTI)
For migrant or refugee women living with family violence

PlunketLine
0800 933 922
Support for parents, including mothers experiencing post-natal depression

Emerge Aotearoa
(09) 470 3530 (Northland) (09) 265 0255 (Auckland) (04) 589 9442 (Midland)   (03) 371 5599 (Wellington) (07) 579 9020 (Christchurch)
Provides a wide range of community-based mental health, addiction, disability support.

Rural Support
0800 787 254
For people in rural communities dealing with financial or personal challenges

Refugees as Survivors
0800 472 769 www.rasnz.co.nz
Psychological support for refugees and asylum seekers.

Asian Family Services
0800 862 342
help@asianfamilyservices.nz
Provides professional, confidential support in multiple languages to Asians living in New Zealand, Monday to Friday 9am –8pm
For families, wha-nau and support workers

Skylight
0800 299 100   www.skylight.org.nz
For support through trauma, loss
and grief (9am – 5pm weekdays)

Supporting Families in Mental Illness
0800 732 825 (Northern Region)
0800 555 434 (Central North Island)
0800 876 682 (South Island)
For families and whānau supporting a loved one who has a mental illness.

Le Va
www.leva.co.nz
www.facebook.com/LeVaPasifika
Information and support for Pasifika families on mental health, addiction and suicide prevention.

Victim Support
0800 842 846
24 hour support for people affected by crime, trauma and suicide.

After a Suicide
www.afterasuicide.nz
A website offering practical information and guidance to people who have lost someone to suicide.

Mental Health Foundation
www.mentalhealth.org.nz
For more information about supporting someone in distress, looking after your own mental health and working toward recovery.

AUSTRALIAN SUPPORT

Beyond Blue
beyondblue.org.au   1300 22 4636
Anyone feeling anxiious or depressed

Kids Helpline
Kidshelpline.com.au   1800 55 1800
Counselling for young people aged 5 to25

Mensline Australia
mensline.org.au   1300 78 99 78
Men with emotional or relationship concerns

Open Arms
openarms.gov.au   1800 011 046
Veterans and families counselling

Lifeline
lifeline.org.au   13 11 14
Anyone having a personal crisis

Suicide Call Back Service
suicidecallbackservice.org.au   1300 659 467
Anyone thinking about suicide

UK SUPPORT

Anxiety UK
Charity providing support if you have been diagnosed with an anxiety condition.
Phone: 03444 775 774 (Monday to Friday, 9.30am to 10pm; Saturday to Sunday, 10am to 8pm)
Website: www.anxietyuk.org.uk

Bipolar UK
A charity helping people living with manic depression or bipolar disorder.
Website: www.bipolaruk.org.uk

CALM
The Campaign Against Living Miserably, for men aged 15 to 35.
Phone: 0800 58 58 58 (daily, 5pm to midnight)
Website: www.thecalmzone.net

Men's Health Forum
24/7 stress support for men by text, chat and email.
Website: www.menshealthforum.org.uk

Mental Health Foundation
Provides information and support for anyone with mental health problems or learning disabilities.
Website: www.mentalhealth.org.uk

Mind
Promotes the views and needs of people with mental health problems.
Phone: 0300 123 3393 (Monday to Friday, 9am to 6pm) Website: www.mind.org.uk

No Panic
Offers a course to help overcome your phobia or OCD.
Phone: 0844 967 4848 (daily, 10am to 10pm). Calls cost 5p per minute plus your phone provider's Access Charge. Website: www.nopanic.org.uk

OCD Action
Support for people with OCD. Includes information on treatment and online resources.
Phone: 0845 390 6232 (Monday to Friday, 9.30am to 5pm). Calls cost 5p per minute plus your phone provider's Access Charge
Website: www.ocdaction.org.uk

OCD UK
A charity run by people with OCD, for people with OCD. Includes facts, news and treatments.
Phone: 0333 212 7890 (Monday to Friday, 9am to 5pm) Website: www.ocduk.org

PAPYRUS

Young suicide prevention society.
Phone: HOPELINEUK 0800 068 4141 (Monday to Friday, 10am to 10pm, and 2pm to 10pm on weekends and bank holidays)
Website: www.papyrus-uk.org

Rethink Mental Illness

Support and advice for people living with mental illness.
Phone: 0300 5000 927 (Monday to Friday, 9.30am to 4pm) Website: www.rethink.org

Samaritans

Confidential support for people experiencing feelings of distress or despair.
Phone: 116 123 (free 24-hour helpline)
Website: www.samaritans.org.uk

SANE

Emotional support, information and guidance for people affected by mental illness, their families and carers.
SANEline: 0300 304 7000 (daily, 4.30pm to 10.30pm)
Textcare: comfort and care via text message, sent when the person needs it most: www.sane.org.uk/textcare
Peer support forum: www.sane.org.uk/supportforum
Website: www.sane.org.uk/support

YoungMinds

Information on child and adolescent mental health. Services for parents and professionals.
Phone: Parents' helpline 0808 802 5544 (Monday to Friday, 9.30am to 4pm)
Website: www.youngminds.org.uk

ABUSE (CHILD, SEXUAL, DOMESTIC VIOLENCE)

NSPCC

Children's charity dedicated to ending child abuse and child cruelty.
Phone: 0800 1111 for Childline for children (24-hour helpline)
0808 800 5000 for adults concerned about a child (24-hour helpline) Website: www.nspcc.org.uk

Refuge

Advice on dealing with domestic violence.
Phone: 0808 2000 247 (24-hour helpline)
Website: www.refuge.org.uk
Addiction (drugs, alcohol, gambling)

Alcoholics Anonymous

Phone: 0800 917 7650 (24-hour helpline)
Website: www.alcoholics-anonymous.org.uk

National Gambling Helpline

Phone: 0808 8020 133 (daily, 8am to midnight)
Website: www.begambleaware.org

Narcotics Anonymous

Phone: 0300 999 1212 (daily, 10am to midnight)
Website: www.ukna.org

Alzheimer's

Alzheimer's Society
Provides information on dementia, including factsheets and helplines.
Phone: 0333 150 3456 (Monday to Friday, 9am to 5pm and 10am to 4pm on weekends)
Website: www.alzheimers.org.uk

BEREAVEMENT

Cruse Bereavement Care

Phone: 0808 808 1677 (Monday to Friday, 9am to 5pm) Website: www.cruse.org.uk

CRIME VICTIMS

Rape Crisis

To find your local services phone: 0808 802 9999 (daily, 12pm to 2.30pm and 7pm to 9.30pm)
Website: www.rapecrisis.org.uk

Victim Support

Phone: 0808 168 9111 (24-hour helpline)
Website: www.victimsupport.org

EATING DISORDERS

Beat

Phone: 0808 801 0677 (adults) or 0808 801 0711 (for under-18s) Website: www.b-eat.co.uk

LEARNING DISABILITIES

Mencap

Charity working with people with a learning disability, their families and carers.
Phone: 0808 808 1111 (Monday to Friday, 9am to 5pm) Website: www.mencap.org.uk

PARENTING

Family Lives

Advice on all aspects of parenting, including dealing with bullying.
Phone: 0808 800 2222 (Monday to Friday, 9am to 9pm and Saturday to Sunday, 10am to 3pm)
Website: www.familylives.org.uk

RELATIONSHIPS

Relate

The UK's largest provider of relationship support.
Website: www.relate.org.uk